Advance Praise for *FedEx Delivers*

As someone who is committed to infusing nonprofit organizations and the public sector with dynamism and creativity that animates great organizations, I'm always on the lookout for books to help us do that. From the moment I started reading *FedEx Delivers*, I knew I had found just such a book.

GAYLE ROSE
Cofounder, Women's Foundation for a Greater Memphis

Madan manages to capture the concepts from soft sciences and transform them into hard principles validated by real-world examples from FedEx. A must-read for managers looking for proven ideas to unleash employees' creativity and commitment.

JOHN SANTI
Managing Director
Stanford Group Company

Want some great ideas for beating the competition tomorrow and the day after? Madan Birla describes the management architecture and specific innovations FedEx uses to beat its competitors year after year. FedEx delivers with its performance culture, and so does this book.

RICHARD DAFT
Brownlee O. Currey Jr., Professor of Management,
Vanderbilt University Author, *Fusion Leadership* and
The Leadership Experience

Innovation isn't just about having great ideas. It's about developing them, leading with vision, and executing tenaciously. Madan Birla clearly understands this and provides a window into an iconic company that created an industry by shattering a customer compromise and continuing to raise the bar through innovation.

STEVE PRESTON
Executive Vice President, Strategic Services
ServiceMaster

FedEx Delivers tells a clear, compelling story about the leadership practices that contributed so mightily to the company's phenomenal success. Founder and

CEO Fred Smith, a visionary and inspiring leader, comes across as a self-effacing business hero, a rarity in today's celebrity-saturated culture.

JOHN O'NEIL
President, The Center for Leadership Renewal
Author, *Paradox of Success*

Provides an easy-to-follow road map for building an innovation and performance culture.

RAM NOMULA
Executive Vice President, Manufacturing Services
Technicolor Home Entertainment Services

Madan delivers an insightful insider's view in helping us understand what makes FedEx tick and how you can use that for your enterprise. *FedEx Delivers* is a must-read resource for all leaders interested in gaining a competitive edge.

TOM GEGAX
Author, *By the Seat of Your Pants: The No-Nonsense
Business Management Guide*

By telling us stories about the leaders he encountered during his 22 years with FedEx, Birla teaches us five valuable lessons any organization can apply to keep innovating and stay ahead of the competition.

BEN KEDIA
Robert Wang Chair of Excellence in International Business
The University of Memphis

Birla's insights into how FedEx continues to grow and foster this highly recognized innovation culture is a testament to the leadership excellence and employee commitment. *FedEx Delivers* inspires the reader to apply these ideas.

KATHY MAZZANTI
Regional Vice President
Right Management Consultants

I was delighted by Madan's holistic approach to creating an innovation and performance culture that acknowledges the critical role of work/life balance.

ALICE CAMPBELL
Director, Community Relations and Work/Life
Baxter International

FedEx Delivers

FedEx Delivers

How the World's Leading Shipping
Company Keeps Innovating and
Outperforming the Competition

Madan Birla

WILEY

John Wiley & Sons, Inc.

Published by John Wiley & Sons, Inc., Hoboken, New Jersey.
Published simultaneously in Canada.

For general information on our other products and services please contact our Customer Care Department within the United States at (800) 762-2974, outside the United States at (317) 572-3993 or fax (317) 572-4002.

Wiley also publishes its books in a variety of electronic formats. Some content that appears in print may not be available in electronic books. For more information about Wiley products, visit our web site at www.wiley.com.

Library of Congress Cataloging-in-Publication Data:

FedEx delivers : how the world's leading shipping company keeps innovating and outperforming the competition / Madan Birla
   p.   cm.
  Includes bibliographical references and index.
  ISBN-13 978-0-471-71579-5 (cloth)
  ISBN-10 0-471-71579-4 (cloth)
  1. Federal Express Corporation—Management   2. Express service—Management.
 I. Title.
HE5903.F435B56   2005
388′.044—dc22

2004028835

Printed in the United States of America.

10 9 8 7 6 5 4 3 2 1

To family, friends, and FedEx colleagues,
who help me celebrate life in its fullness

Contents

Contents

Preface

Rarely can a person join an organization destined for greatness in the early days of its development and then play a key role in helping it fulfill that destiny. I was presented with such an opportunity when I joined FedEx* in 1979. After I had spent the better part of my career helping FedEx become one of the most successful and admired companies in the world, I retired three years ago and decided to share some of the lessons I had learned. Since then, I have addressed business groups across the country and have acted as an advisor and business consultant. During this period, I have had numerous conversations with top executives from dozens of companies about the factors that make a company grow. In these talks with leaders of businesses both large and small, I have asked the same question:

"What is the one improvement that would enable you to realize your revenue and profit growth goals?"

Here are some of the responses I have heard:

"For us to achieve our top line and bottom line targets in today's highly competitive global economy, we have to *innovate*. We cannot continue to do business the way we have been doing."

From its inception in 1973 until 1994, the company was named Federal Express but was popularly known as FedEx. In 1994, FedEx was officially adopted as the company's name. Following the acquisition of Caliber Systems in 1998, the parent company FDX was created. In 2000, FDX was renamed FedEx Corporation, and the original company handling the express shipments was named FedEx Express. All of my experience, from 1979 through 2001, was with the original company, still by far the largest operating company in the FedEx family. All the examples in the book are based on my experience at the original company. To avoid confusion by using Federal Express, FedEx, and FedEx Express, I simply use the name "FedEx."

"To continue to grow in today's highly competitive economy we have to outthink and outperform the competition. To have a competitive edge, we must have an *innovation edge*."

"In today's economy, there is no such thing as a sustainable competitive advantage. We must tap into the creative potential of each employee and harness it to create an *innovation culture*."

The companies I have visited range from having a few hundred employees to having more than 200,000, and show revenues from $20 million to $20 billion annually. Their products and services include foods, transportation, biotechnology, financial advice, health care, and orthopedic implants. But no matter the size or the product, the senior executives of these companies have one thing in common: They all know that to have a profitable business in the twenty-first century, their companies cannot rely on what they have done well in the past—or even what they are doing well today. To enjoy continued growth and prosperity, businesses must innovate.

In today's business world, *innovation* is a buzzword that often leaves employees worried, confused, and unable to meet unclear expectations. I have written this book to share the leadership practices and support systems that helped FedEx become one of the most successful and high-performance companies of all times.

FedEx Delivers will help you understand not only why innovation is essential, but also how you can make it part of your corporate culture. It provides the tools to develop a culture that actively engages every employee in helping your organization increase market share and profitability. You will learn how to adapt the FedEx model to your unique environment so that your employees will keep asking: What new things can we do in our day-to-day work lives to better serve our customers?

The book presents *a step-by-step blueprint* for building and sustaining an innovation and performance culture. Leaders and organizations can learn how to make creative thinking a part of their company's design and infrastructure instead of stumbling on ideas by chance.

In addition to the managers who use this book to build and sustain an innovation and performance culture, corporate trainers will find that *FedEx Delivers* is an ideal resource for their leadership development programs. Academicians can use *FedEx Delivers* in their classes in leadership, innovation, engineering management, international business, and organization development.

Acknowledgments

I want to express deep appreciation to the people whose encouragement and support made this book possible. First, I want to thank Mike Glenn, Executive Vice President, Market Development and Corporate Communications; and Rob Carter, Executive Vice President and Chief Information Officer; both key drivers of innovation at FedEx, for confirming the wisdom and utility of the innovation and performance culture model on which this book is based.

Then, I must thank Sheila Edmundson Redick for her patience in reading, rereading, and refining the material from the first book proposal to the final manuscript. I also thank Ed Hirsch for his valuable critique and conceptual advice.

My sincere thanks to the following colleagues for being so generous with their time in sharing their FedEx experiences: Roger Albee, Shawn Allison, Henry Bartosch, Marco Chan, Kay Coop, Harry Dalton, Matt DiGiovanna, Kewal Gupta, Don Hardy, Arun Kulkarni, Arun Kumar, Bonnie McKeever, Mike Moss, Karen O'Malley, Jim Petrie, Steve Priddy, Jack Roberts, Gloria Sangster-Fort, Steve Stapleton, Mike Staunton, Norm Wilcox, and Linda Wolowicz.

Bob Bennett, Kirk Bobo, Arun Kumtha, Sarah Meyerrose, Larry Papasan, Robin Robinson, and Gayle Rose took time from their busy schedules to read chapter drafts and provide valuable suggestions. Rodney McElroy provided help with the graphics.

John Willig, my literary agent, deserves special thanks for his counsel at critical steps during the development of the book. Matt Holt and Shannon Vargo at John Wiley & Sons, Inc. gave me their above-and-beyond editorial support. Shannon's insightful comments have been very helpful in making the material flow smoothly.

Finally, I convey my deepest appreciation to Fred Smith, founder and CEO of FedEx, for having the courage to pursue his vision through difficult times in the company's early days. He created an opportunity for thousands of people like me to be part of a great global business success story. We, the veterans of FedEx, proudly share our experiences with future generations.

About the Author

Madan Birla is a veteran of the "hard" side of business. In his 22 years at FedEx, he was Managing Director of System Form Engineering (Long-Range Operations and Facilities Planning) and Materials and Resource Planning before being named Managing Director and Preceptor in the company's Leadership Institute. For eight years as a member of the Long-Range Planning Committee, he worked closely with Fred Smith and the senior management team in evaluating strategic *what-ifs*. At the FedEx Leadership Institute, he was a facilitator of Innovation, Leadership, and Life Balance courses for all levels of management throughout the world. For the past three years, he has been advising executives on how to encourage employee creativity and commitment to build a culture of innovation and performance.

His life experiences in two rich cultures, East and West, and his broad educational background have prepared him to meld ideas from engineering, business, and psychology to develop comprehensive Leading for Innovation models. He completed his undergraduate work in mechanical engineering at the Birla Institute of Technology and Science in Pilani, India. Following that, he enrolled at the Illinois Institute of Technology (IIT) in Chicago, Illinois, where he received his master of science degree in industrial engineering. After graduating, he joined RCA Records in Indianapolis, Indiana. While in Indianapolis, he did graduate work in business at Butler University. After moving to Memphis to join FedEx, he received a master of science degree in counseling from the University of Memphis.

Author (Left) Receiving His Second Five Star Award, the Highest Recognition for Leadership Excellence at FedEx, from Fred Smith, Founder and CEO of FedEx

He has received many awards, including membership in Alpha Pi Mu, the Industrial Engineering Honor Society; he was named as an Honorary Citizen of the city of Indianapolis for his community involvement; and he received Five Star Awards, the highest recognition for Leadership Excellence at FedEx.

He is a regular speaker at professional and business group meetings including the Society of Human Resource Management (SHRM) Global Human Resource Forums in New York and Monterey, California; Alliance of Work/Life Professionals, annual conference in New Orleans, and chapter meetings in Chicago, St. Louis, and Santa Barbara; American Management Association, Executive

Forums in New York, Chicago, and San Francisco; Tennessee Leadership Conference and Leadership Academy, Illinois Institute of Technology, Chicago, Illinois.

He is actively involved in volunteer work for the community. He led the effort to establish the Indian Community Fund for Greater Memphis, which funded the Gandhi exhibit at the National Civil Rights Museum in Memphis and "Windows to the World," an interactive educational exhibit at the Children's Museum of Memphis, among other projects. He developed long-range plans for the Church Health Center (serving working poor), Friends for Life (serving the HIV/AIDS affected population), and the Tipton County Commission on Aging (serving seniors). He lives with his wife Shashi in Collierville, Tennessee, and has two grown children who live in New York and Chicago.

Introduction

FedEx Delivers: How the World's Leading Shipping Company Keeps Innovating and Outperforming the Competition explores in detail the leadership philosophy and practices responsible for FedEx's phenomenal growth. This book's uniquely practical approach gives readers the processes and tools that FedEx has used to become a market leader.

Chapter 1 takes the mystery out of innovation by breaking it down into three steps—generation, acceptance, and implementation of ideas. Typically, employees think of innovation only in terms of the first step—coming up with a unique idea. Once they understand that acceptance and implementation are also essential, they realize that their contribution in those steps is equally important.

The second chapter explores the premise that innovation is not something a person or company does just once. To sustain a competitive advantage, businesses must maintain an environment that encourages new ideas. Fred Smith had a new concept when he launched the company, but he achieved lasting success because the business continued to adapt to the changing business environment. Building and sustaining an innovation culture is a journey.

The third chapter asks the question, "If business leaders recognize the need for innovation, why is it that only a few succeed in that quest?" What exactly are the roadblocks to innovation? The five most common obstacles are discussed.

Chapter 4 develops a mental model of innovation by exploring when the mind is in the best position to generate, accept, and implement creative ideas. For this process to flourish, the mind must be engaged, growing, secure, collaborative, and committed. This chapter defines the five leadership responsibilities associated with creating these conditions.

The remaining chapters of the book discuss in detail the practices and organizational support systems needed to fulfill each of the five leadership responsibilities. Each practice is illustrated by firsthand examples from FedEx. Chapter 5 describes the four leadership practices used at FedEx to engage and involve all their employees. Although a car engine may be running, the car will not move forward unless the engine is engaged. Similarly, for an organization to grow and move forward, employees have to be engaged in the enterprise.

The four leadership practices and organizational support systems that help employees update and expand their knowledge bases are presented in Chapter 6. The mind generates creative ideas by making connections between seemingly unrelated variables. The creative impulse rests on seeing new possibilities and new combinations. For the mind to generate creative ideas, it must either connect existing dots (one's knowledge base) in new ways or acquire and connect new dots.

Chapter 7 focuses on the four leadership practices used at FedEx to create a secure environment for the expression and acceptance of ideas. Creative thoughts are rarely refined and ready to implement at the outset. They need to be developed. For many, sharing a raw idea is unnerving: What will management think? Could I be reprimanded if my suggestion doesn't mesh with my supervisor's? Is it stupid? These questions and fears are all very real in today's business culture, leading many employees to keep their ideas to themselves—a major hurdle in the quest for innovation. Employees have to feel secure to express their ideas. Managers have to feel secure to accept new ideas, especially ones that are different from their own views.

Before any creative idea can be implemented, it must be made palatable to the many people it will affect. Depending on its scope, an idea and the resulting change may affect multiple departments in the organization. Therefore, complete development and refinement of the raw idea demand active collaboration throughout all the affected areas.

Chapter 8 includes four leadership practices that encourage collaboration across departments and disciplines. Active collaboration not only ensures full evaluation and development of the idea but also positions the organization to successfully implement it. When people from different backgrounds, departments, and perspectives work together to refine a new idea, the result is likely to be far better than what any one of them would have come up with alone.

Chapter 9 presents proven leadership practices for tapping employees' commitment, a must for successful implementation of developed ideas. Since anything truly creative results in change, this personal commitment helps overcome employees' natural reluctance to embrace new ideas. It is the employees' commitment at all levels of the organization that has made it possible for FedEx to deliver day-in and day-out on its promise to customers around the world.

Chapter 1

Innovating and Outperforming the Competition

Our vast progress in transportation, past and future, is only a symbol of the progress that is possible by constantly striving toward new horizons in every human activity. Who can say what new horizons lie before us if we can but maintain the initiative and develop the imagination to penetrate them—to the end that greater degrees of well being may be enjoyed by everyone, everywhere.

—Alfred P. Sloan Jr.

CREATING A NEW INDUSTRY . . .

On FedEx's first night of operation, April 17, 1973, a small group of people stood around a makeshift system and sorted 186 packages. They then loaded them onto 14 small planes that promptly took off for 25 cities across the United States. On that night, FedEx became the first transportation company dedicated to overnight express package delivery. Thirty-two years later, FedEx handles over five million packages every day serving 215 countries around the globe.

FedEx's revenue grew from just $6 million in 1973 to over $24 billion in 2004. In 1983, it was the first company to grow to $1 billion within the first 10 years of its existence, without acquisitions. During the first three years of its operation (1973–1975), FedEx lost over $29 million as it built its infrastructure and established the network that would allow it to start making a profit. For the past three years (2002–2004), its net income has been over $2.3 billion.

Today's FedEx, which has constantly evolved to meet customer needs, consists of four operating companies connecting the global economy with a full range of transportation, information, and supply chain services. This change and growth did not happen overnight. The factors that contributed to FedEx's phenomenal success included developing customized business solutions. One example is FedEx's relationship with Hewlett-Packard. In the fast-changing computer industry with new models coming out every month, HP realized that any computer stored in a warehouse runs the risk of becoming obsolete. FedEx and Hewlett-Packard worked together to develop a supply chain solution that eliminated the warehousing of HP's industry-leading notebook PCs. The notebooks were shipped directly from the manufacturing facilities in China to homes and businesses throughout North America in just two to three working days.

Over the past five years, FedEx's stock price has doubled. During the same period, the stock price of its main competitor, United Parcel Service (UPS) increased by only 15 percent, and the Standard & Poor's 500 fell by 20 percent. FedEx has been recognized as one of the 100 Best Companies to Work for in America (*Fortune*, 1998–2004) and also as one of America's Most Admired Companies (2001–2004).

. . . BY TAPPING EMPLOYEES' CREATIVITY AND COMMITMENT

Before starting FedEx, Fred Smith hired consultants to do a feasibility study and help develop his business idea into a detailed business plan. The consultants estimated the total market potential for air freight to be around $1 billion. Today, FedEx's share of the express transportation industry is over $17 billion. What allowed FedEx not only to create the express industry and grow the overall market, but to continue to enjoy a dominant market share?

FedEx became an international powerhouse and one of the most trusted global brands by implementing leadership practices that tapped into the discretionary effort, creativity, and commitment of its employees at all levels of the organization — the foundation of a thriving innovation and performance culture. True, Fred Smith had the original business idea, but it was the creativity and commitment of employees that turned it into a successful business. The employees of FedEx have designed and delivered unique customer value propositions (what customers value) that have kept FedEx one step ahead of the competition.

Even though the managers at FedEx did not consciously set out to build and sustain an innovation culture, that is precisely what they accomplished. The open and supportive environment allowed employees at all levels in the organization to be part of the innovation process. The day-to-day leadership practices and behaviors and the company's organizational support systems have been keys to FedEx's phenomenal growth.

This book provides a model, or a framework, that explains how these leadership practices and organizational support systems, working together, built and sustained the FedEx's innovation and performance culture.

There is no company manual entitled *The FedEx Way: How to Build and Sustain an Innovation Culture.* The book you are reading is based on FedEx managers' *firsthand experiences and interpretation* of those experiences in the context of the innovation culture model and the three-step process (generation, acceptance, implementation).

Business leaders also should keep in mind that it is neither feasible nor practical to adopt principles and practices "lock, stock, and barrel" from another organization and try to fit them into their own existing culture because *each organization is unique.*

Some organizations may already apply some of the leadership practices that promote innovation but do not get the collective benefit—a thriving innovation culture—because some of the pieces may be missing. The goal is to help managers *identify and implement* the missing piece(s) to actively engage every employee in the innovation process.

The leadership practices and support systems discussed in this book are not unique to FedEx; they have proven to be equally effective in other organizations.

DEFINING CREATIVITY IN THE BUSINESS WORLD

Two key terms are often used interchangeably—creativity and innovation. People normally associate creativity with artistic endeavors—Monet, Picasso, Michelangelo, and Mozart, the artist's studio, the visual arts, or the performing arts. In the context of the business world, I define *creativity* as the process of *generating ideas* that will help the organization become more competitive in the marketplace. Business creativity is generating ideas that will improve the customer experience, increase revenue and market share, or improve efficiency. The thought process uses imagination just as artists do: "What if . . . ?" What if we make this change in our business strategy, product design, manufacturing process, distribution process, billing system, accounting system, and so on?

Walt Disney, after seeing run-down rides and bored adults during a visit to an amusement park with his daughter, thought, "What if there was a place where kids and adults could play together?"

Similarly Sam Walton, CEO of Wal-Mart, asked, "What if we connect the cash register to the inventory planning systems and substantially reduce the cost of doing business?"

After realizing that there was a growing demand for a time-definite express mode of transportation for shipping high-priority, time-sensitive cargo such as computer parts, critical documents, medicines, and electronics, Fred Smith thought, "What if we develop an airline dedicated to providing overnight express service to meet this growing need?" He went one step further and thought, "What if this airline used the hub-and-spoke system?"

Initially, Fred developed and proposed the hub-and-spoke system to the Federal Reserve System for overnight delivery of checks between their 36 locations around the country. At that time, clearing checks used to take anywhere from one to four days. This created a huge *float*, that is, checks written and presented for deposit but not yet cleared and credited in the recipients' accounts. The overnight express system would have eliminated the float. The word "Federal" in the company's original name came from the proposal to carry the Federal Reserve's checks and "Express" represented the speed with which the new company would carry them.

Creativity in the business world means exploring what ifs—taking time to seek the connection between seemingly unrelated variables, to see other possibilities, and to look at the bigger picture when making decisions. Fred Smith thought out his ideas while he wrote his now-famous Yale term paper. When he was raising venture capital in the early 1970s to start FedEx, a shipper could send a critical package using passenger airlines.

Passenger airlines, for many reasons, did not always guarantee a time-definite and cost-effective service. First, because the primary goal of the passenger airlines was flying passengers, the departure and arrival schedules were built around the needs of the passengers. A flight might not be scheduled to leave at the time a customer wanted to ship a package. Or a flight may not have been scheduled to the destination the package needed to reach, or there might not have been a flight scheduled to arrive at the time the shipment needed to be there. Second, customers had to take packages to the airport because the airlines did not provide pickup service. The only way to avoid that problem was to have a third party pick up the package and transport it to the airport, which added substantially to the shipping cost.

A similar situation existed at the destination end. On arrival, the recipient or a designee had to pick up the package and deliver to the final destination. In general, the handling systems of the passenger airlines were designed to serve the passengers. Processing packages in an expeditious manner was not part of the design.

Fred's creative idea substantially improved on the then standard express transportation service by making custodial control and "door-to-door" service part of the design of his proposed venture.

THE THREE-STEP INNOVATION PROCESS

Whereas creativity deals solely with the generation of ideas by exploring what if scenarios, innovation starts with creative ideas but takes the process two steps further. As Rosabeth Moss Kanter says in her landmark book, *The Change Masters*, "innovation is the generation, acceptance, and implementation of new ideas, processes, products or services. It can thus occur in any part of a corporation, and it can involve creative use as well as original invention. Application and implementation are central to this definition; it involves the capacity to change or adapt." Innovation is the act of introducing something new. Innovation is applied creativity.

The process involves an increasing number of people as it moves through the three steps:

Step One: Individuals freely generate and express creative ideas.

Step Two: A small group composed of people in departments and disciplines affected by the idea(s), accept and work collaboratively to develop the raw idea(s) into sound business plans.

Step Three: A much larger group—in some cases the whole organization, depending on the scope—adopts the idea(s) and works to develop and implement it.

Walt Disney, Fred Smith, and Sam Walton had original ideas. But it required people from various disciplines to shape those raw ideas into viable business plans. And it required an even greater number (entire organizations) to successfully implement the business plans. Disney, Smith, and Walton understood that humans are inherently creative beings and have a psychological need to make a difference and to be part of a winning team. As leaders, they developed an environment in which the employees could unleash their potential and be part of the innovation process. The leaders and their employees together created truly world-class organizations.

Typically, employees think innovation means coming up with a unique idea. That's why it's so important to let employees know that they are also making valuable contributions when they are being open to new ideas and putting them into practice. Employees who help implement new ideas are playing a vital role because great results require great ideas and great implementation (execution).

The successful implementation step is sometimes more important than the generation and acceptance of ideas. On more than one occasion, I have witnessed a well-implemented mediocre idea that has produced great results. I have witnessed poorly implemented great ideas that produced poor results. But the worst results I have seen are great ideas that were not accepted and implemented at all. This is where companies feel the negative effects of missed opportunities for increasing the market share, reducing the cost of doing business, or improving the customer experience as their competition moves ahead of the pack.

IMPLEMENTATION IS KEY

Top executives have plenty of ideas and understand the importance of implementing them, but few have figured out how to do so, according to two new surveys. A recent survey of 350 executives in the United States and a similar polling of business leaders in the United Kingdom both sponsored by management and technology services firm Accenture suggest that:

- More than half of the executives polled say innovation is one of the five most important factors in building competitive advantage, and 10 percent say it is the most important factor.
- More than 75 percent of top managers say their people generate enough good ideas.
- Only 10 percent of executives say their organization excels at innovation, and 46 percent say they implement fewer than 20 percent of their promising ideas.

"The best companies have an innovation culture," says Peter Cheese, a managing partner at Accenture in London.

—From "Great Ideas Abound, But Implementation Lags," *HR Magazine*, March 2003

In early 1980, a few months after I started working at FedEx, the company was guaranteeing overnight delivery by noon. As part of my new employee orientation, I put on a FedEx courier uniform and rode all day with Susan, a courier in Dallas, while she picked up and delivered packages. That day, Susan completed her deliveries by 11:15 A.M. As soon as she finished, Susan called the other couriers in her part of town to see if they needed help. Bill, another courier, radioed back that he could use some help. Susan asked where he was headed for his next delivery stop, and we met him at a Walgreens drugstore close to his stop. We transferred some packages from Bill's van to Susan's van and delivered the packages. With this last-minute collaboration, all packages were delivered on time that morning.

I was completely amazed.

At RCA Records (my place of employment for 10 years before joining FedEx), an employee on a shift who completed his production quota earlier than his shift schedule would just sit in the break room until it was time to clock out; I was surprised at the unfamiliar practices of the FedEx employees. While riding along with Susan, I asked if the other employees did the same thing she had done for Bill when they completed their deliveries. She looked at me with an expression that conveyed, "Why would you even ask such a question?" and replied, "Of course, Bill and other couriers have helped me out many times when I was struggling to make all my deliveries on time. We all know from experience that on a given day some routes will be heavier than the others. Also, there may be traffic problems in some part of town. Everybody's goal in the Dallas pickup and delivery operations is the same—on-time delivery to our customers every day."

This experience and others like it in the first few months of my arrival convinced me that the unique culture at FedEx influenced employees to go above and beyond the call of duty to make sure the company kept its promise to its customers.

PSP PHILOSOPHY

In the first week at FedEx, I attended an all-day orientation session conducted by the human resources department. The human resources manager talked a lot about FedEx's PSP (People, Service, Profit) culture and its "People First" philosophy. Put simply, the PSP culture means that FedEx puts its people (employees) first in everything it does, and as a result, FedEx employees put the customer first in everything they do.

FedEx has to rely on employees for crisp execution of its operating plans for the pickup and delivery of five million packages worldwide daily. Even though operations and schedules are planned extensively, the reality is that on a given day there will be delays in the system (flight delays because of bad weather, traffic delays in the city because of construction and other uncontrollable factors, etc.). Overcoming these problems comes down to the frontline employees, who must adapt to the disruptions and ensure FedEx meets its service commitments. Another metaphor used to explain the PSP culture was a three-legged stool. Each of the three legs is equally important. And each leg must be equally strong for the stool to be stable. For FedEx to be healthy and successful, all three elements of the PSP culture had to be strong. If you treat people well, they will be more inclined to provide excellent service, which will generate profits that benefit everyone.

Within four months of joining FedEx, I received a letter from Fred Smith, announcing a special 3 percent raise for all employees. The letter made it clear to us that it was because of our efforts in providing superior service that the company's financial picture was much brighter. Although we did not get special raises after that, FedEx's profit sharing plan has ensured that employees continue to benefit from the company's success. Based on the company's profitability, all employees receive a check before Christmas as part of the current profit-sharing plan. At the end of the fiscal year, another distribution is made as part of the deferred profit-sharing plan. This amount is deposited into employees' deferred profit-sharing accounts. You will have to design your program based on the reality of your business environment. The goal is to tie personal well-being with the company's overall performance.

My department was responsible for developing long-range operations and facilities plans for FedEx locations worldwide. I rode with couriers in Tokyo, Hong Kong, Bombay, and other cities. My experience riding with Susan—observing the mutually respectful interactions between the customers and the couriers—confirmed for me the key role of the PSP culture and the People First philosophy in helping FedEx set the industry standard for customer service and reliability. In my 22 years at FedEx, whenever I went on a business trip, I tried to schedule at least half a day riding with a courier in that city. I found this to be the best way to get a feel for the unique characteristics of that market and the current operating scenario. I observed the same above-and-beyond dedication in employees in every city and country. Leading the people the FedEx Way was producing similar results worldwide.

Many times, friends and business acquaintances have commented, "FedEx employees are the most friendly and customer service oriented employees." A friend of mine in Chicago continually praised employees at the FedEx's Business Service Center close to her office on Michigan Avenue. Once she told me, "Sometimes I'm running late and there is a long line just before the closing time in the evening. But the staff goes out of their way to make sure every person in the line has his or her shipping needs met."

In the following months, I learned much more about the PSP culture and People First philosophy as well as about the critical role managers and employees at all levels play in making it a day-to-day reality. The PSP culture and the People First philosophy are key innovations that have made FedEx the industry leader it is today. Many companies espouse a similar people philosophy on paper in their manuals and annual reports. What sets FedEx apart is the remarkable way it has breathed life into that philosophy.

In the following chapters, I describe not just how FedEx institutionalized the PSP philosophy but how it encourages the leadership practices that support innovation. The genius of PSP was not just the telegraphic and shorthand way the principles were enunciated and communicated, but the metrics that were put in place to measure whether they were working. Accountability was built into the system. Every company has a metric for profit, but FedEx created a measure for people/leadership and another for service from the customer's perspective. Other companies have enlightened practices, but FedEx figured out how to measure the extent to which those practices are being followed. Later chapters show how FedEx created systems to ensure that people (employees and customers) were treated well and that impeccable service would be delivered virtually all the time.

Leading under the PSP philosophy, managers recognized that some people were naturally good at generating ideas. Some people were skilled at working with other departments in further developing the raw ideas. And others were adept at implementing the developed ideas. At different stages of the innovation process, the roles can change. A programmer might not have the knowledge base to generate ideas about the corporate business strategy but certainly would have creative ideas while designing and programming a specific part of the management information system to execute this strategy. With this recognition, the managers encouraged and allowed the employees to play the roles in which they were most successful. Procter & Gamble's CEO, A. G. Lafley said it well:

> People get as much credit for giving good ideas as for receiving them.
>
> —A. G. Lafley, CEO, "Innovation Special,"
> *Fortune*, May 31, 2004

And the result:

> Since he took over in the summer of 2000, operating income, adjusted for extraordinary gains and charges, is up an average of 17 percent. The stock price has nearly doubled. Lafley brought a whole lot of creativity and rigor to P&G's innovation process, a tough thing to do in the notoriously rule-bound culture. During the past two years, P&G has raised its new-product hit rate

(the percentage of new entries that deliver a return above the cost of capital) from 70 percent to 90 percent. That's terrific in an industry where half of new products fail within 12 months, according to market-research firm Information Resources.

— Story by Patricia Sellers, "Innovation Special," *Fortune*, May 31, 2004

I also share how Susan and other individuals helped build FedEx into one of the world's most trusted global brands. It is the brand that people associate with on-time performance, reliability, *innovation*, and customer-driven technology.

POSITIVE PACKAGE TRACKING AND ON-TIME GUARANTEE

FedEx was founded on the idea of meeting time-definite express transportation needs, but it really took off when Fred Smith realized and verbalized that the company was not in the transportation business but in the peace-of-mind business. The new business purpose resulted in the development and implementation of innovative package tracking systems designed to let customers know exactly where their packages were and when they arrived at their final destinations. On the surface, it may appear to be a creative application of the existing technologies. But a deeper look reveals the involvement of hundreds of people in developing the idea and the entire organization in implementing it. The successful implementation of the expanding business models required innovative thinking at all levels of the organization.

I called Harry Dalton, who was Director, Systems Engineering & Design when the project began and later was Vice President, Strategic Integrated Systems. I asked him, as project leader for this industry-changing innovation, to discuss the details surrounding

FedEx's implementation of the tracking system. I told him I wanted to learn about it from the person who made it all happen. To that, Harry responded, "You are being too kind. I had lots of good people working with me."

Here's a sampling of our exchange:

Q: Looking back on your experience from a big picture perspective, what were the keys to success for this project?

A: Off the top of my head, I'd say it came down to five things:

1. A clear definition of the project objective, which was to develop and implement a positive tracking system.
2. Thorough understanding of the company's operations. (Prior to the leadership role for this project, Harry was director of operations in the Mid-Atlantic district.)
3. A keen understanding of what the information needs were from the customer standpoint.
4. High-level project sponsorship. (Throughout the project's duration, Harry reported to the president of the company.)
5. Technical expertise within my staff to leverage what we were asking the vendors to do.

Q: Walk me through the detailed steps of developing and implementing this trailblazing Innovation.

A: We hired smart people and gave them interesting work. We made sure they all knew that the work they were doing was going to make FedEx the first transportation company to offer positive tracking. Engineers like these types of challenges.

The team had complete freedom to explore options for how best to meet this challenge. You have to remember this began almost 25 years ago when the available technology was not what it is today. There were no off-the-shelf portable scanners. The bar code printing technology was not what it is today. At that time, we couldn't print a readable sequential bar code on the seven-part airway bills and we needed them by millions. We worked with Mead, 3M, and Standard Register for the bar code printing technology. Our bar code was much different than what they were using in grocery stores.

The first thing the group did was to define the requirements and possible operating scenarios. We regularly scheduled all-team breakfast meetings during which everyone had a chance to voice their opinions and ask questions. One of the products we tested at six stations in 1981, and that provided initial rollout, was the Norand scanning device. We continued to meet with vendors and described our need for smaller, more powerful devices. Most of them left the meetings laughing. Finally, we found a vendor located in Charlotte, North Carolina, who was interested in working with us. We tested several different systems. The goal was to develop and implement station-to-station positive tracking initially and then to drive the technology to expand to door-to-door tracking. The tests were successful, and by February 1982, we had 100 percent, systemwide coverage.

During the development phase, we were asked to give a demonstration at the board of directors meeting. We actually were able to track a random package from the previous night into the board room. We were able to positively track the package leaving the origin station the night before and arriving at the destination station . . . 22 years ago!

Throughout the development and testing process, we made regular presentations at each of the director's and vice president's staff meetings and all employee meetings to update them on what was working and what was not working. At every meeting, we asked for feedback. Fred Smith regularly invited us to present updates at the senior officers' meetings. We received tremendous support from the corporate communications department. This ongoing communication and involvement of operations people in the development and testing phase were keys to acceptance and successful implementation in the field.

In 1985, we started testing the invention that came to be called the SuperTracker® and we were able to show exactly who signed for each package. This handheld scanning device allowed us to scan packages at every stage in the pickup and delivery process. Now we could tell exactly where the package was at any point in time, whether at the station, in the courier van, or delivered. There were many challenges and modifications along the way before we had a SuperTracker that met our operational needs. We were pushing the envelope of available technology. We trained 26,000 employees to use this technology between November 1985 and May 1986, at which time the rollout was completed.

Generous recognition of the team members was also a key factor in keeping the group motivated. The project lasted more than four years. At senior officers' meetings, I would ask the team members to make the presentation. I made sure they got the credit. Senior management recognized them by presenting several of them with the Five-Star Award, the highest award for recognizing creativity and leadership excellence at FedEx.

This innovation allowed us to introduce other operation- and service-enhancing improvements, such as the courier printer. Before this printer, which produces labels, the courier had to write a routing code on the package with a marking pen. The courier printer not only automated that function but improved the accuracy. The machine printed the sorting codes that in turn allowed us to introduce automated sorting in the hubs.

The design and implementation of the SuperTracker system shows the importance of each of the three steps of the innovation process—generation, acceptance, and implementation. The

FIGURE 1.1 Beetle Bailey Cartoon. © Reprinted with permission of King Features Syndicate.

cartoon strip in Figure 1.1 provides another illustration of how this works. Although it pokes fun at the mundane ways some employees contribute to advances within their organization, anyone who has worked within the bowels of organizations large and small knows how indispensable all those contributions really are. Chapter 2 discusses in detail the culture that FedEx developed to ensure that all employees would contribute to the innovation process.

Chapter 2

FedEx's Innovation Journey

Looking back on 25 years at the forefront of a dynamic and evolving industry, two things have remained constant at FedEx: change, and the ability and willingness of our employees to embrace change on behalf of our customers.

— Fred Smith, Founder and CEO, FedEx

Innovation is not something a person or company does just once. To sustain a competitive advantage, businesses must continually innovate. Fred Smith's idea launched the company, but the business grew and became successful because it continued to innovate. Building and maintaining an innovation culture is a journey.

We all know of once hugely successful companies like Polaroid, Wang, Pan Am, Kmart, Xerox, and TWA that started with innovative products or services but are no longer around, or are a fraction of the size they once were. In today's economy, there is no such thing as a *sustainable* competitive advantage. The frenetic pace of technological changes, increased globalization, and relentless shifts in consumer tastes all demand that companies continually ask: "What could we be doing differently to enhance our competitive edge?" and "What could we be doing differently to serve our customers better?" This ongoing internal dialogue needs to take place at all levels of the organization, from executives who contemplate the business purpose to the front-line workers who enact the business processes.

MY VANTAGE POINT ON THIS EXCITING JOURNEY

Sometime in September 1979, I noticed an advertisement in the *Wall Street Journal* for the position of Manager of Materials and Warehouse Planning at Federal Express in Memphis, Tennessee. I had joined RCA after receiving an MS in industrial engineering from the Illinois Institute of Technology in Chicago. My wife and I were living in Indianapolis, where we had a large circle of friends; our son had just started first grade; and we had just moved into a brand-new, custom-built house. I was in the middle of my night school MBA program at Butler University.

But two things intrigued me about the Federal Express job: (1) the challenge of joining a young company and (2) the possibility of moving to a warmer region. My wife and I had learned to cope with the cold, snowy winters, but we both longed for a milder climate. After sending my resume, I received a call asking me to meet Dennis Sweeney, Federal Express's Director of Distribution Services, for breakfast at the Indianapolis Airport Hilton.

I did not know much about Federal Express—just what I had seen in their funny TV commercials, an "absolutely positively overnight" package delivery company. So one of my first questions to Dennis was, "You're a service company and don't really manufacture anything. Why do you need a materials manager?" My experience and understanding up to that point was that typically a materials manager makes sure that manufacturing operations have the right materials at the right place and at the right time to produce the scheduled products. Dennis explained that Federal Express needed a wide variety of materials both internally for its various operating divisions, and externally for its customers. The materials to support the internal operations ranged from spare parts for the airplanes to the uniforms for the delivery couriers. Externally, materials included airway bills and packaging supplies.

In addition to explaining the duties and responsibilities of the advertised position, Sweeney spent quite a bit of time telling me about the tremendous growth the company had experienced in its first six years as well as the plans for even greater expansion in the near future. A few weeks later, I was invited to visit Memphis for an interview. I was offered the job in November, and in December 1979, I joined Federal Express as Manager of Materials and Warehouse Planning.

In just a few weeks at FedEx, I noticed big differences between the environment and culture at RCA and my new employer. Both the RCA Corporation and the Records division were old, established companies. At RCA Records, the business had matured and was hardly growing. The pace of life at work was slow and steady, with infrequent changes. At RCA as a member of the Indianapolis management team, I often traveled to corporate headquarters in New York for meetings. The interaction with the executive management at the corporate level in RCA was formal and hierarchical. At FedEx, changes were taking place every week. The pace of life was fast. There was excitement in the air. There was a sense of urgency, and everyone was fully engaged in the enterprise. FedEx executive management was accessible. It was not unusual for Fred or other senior officers to stop by and say hello to employees at any of the 20 FedEx office buildings around the Memphis airport.

In 1986, I was promoted to Managing Director of Materials and Resource Planning. After 10 years, the materials planning department was running smoothly. Department managers and the employees were well trained. The planning systems had been upgraded. I started to seek assignments outside my direct areas of responsibility including leading a quality action team (QAT) to improve the long-range planning process. I thoroughly enjoyed these assignments and mentioned to my boss, Ken Willoughby, Vice President in the Central Support Services Division, that I was ready for a new challenge. He asked me if I would be interested in System Form Engineering, a key department in the long-range planning process and worldwide facilities plans. The assignments ranged from generating and evaluating innovative operating scenarios for handling the projected global business growth to deciding the best geographic locations for national and regional sorting facilities around the world.

After nine years as Managing Director of System Form Engineering, I was nominated and selected to be a Managing Director/Preceptor (facilitator) in the FedEx Leadership Institute. The Leadership Institute was established in the early 1980s to train newly promoted managers, senior managers, and managing directors. During my three-year tenure, I facilitated leadership development classes for all levels of management around the world.

GROWTH DURING THIS INNOVATION JOURNEY

From 1979 to 2001, FedEx passed the following milestones:

- Growth in revenue from $400 million to $22 billion
- Growth in aircraft fleet from 60 to 600 planes
- Increase in average daily shipment volume from 60,000 to 4.7 million
- Increase in employees from 7,000 to 200,000
- Expansion in countries served from one (United States) to 215
- *Fortune:* World's Most Admired Companies
- "Best/Top Places to Work": America, Canada, India, Brazil, Asia
- *Financial Times:* World's Most Respected Companies
- First company to hit $1 billion in 10 years (May 1983) from internal growth, without acquisitions

These achievements become even more impressive once you understand the inherent demands and complexities of this business.

THE NUTS AND BOLTS OF FEDEX'S OPERATIONS

The following list traces the journey of a domestic express package through the system:

- Package is ready for shipment. Customer calls FedEx and requests a pickup.
- A message is sent electronically to the courier responsible for the route where the customer is located.
- Courier picks up the package and transports it to the city station at the scheduled time.
- Packages are unloaded from the vans, sorted, and loaded into containers at the city station.
- Loaded containers are trucked to the city airport, again at a scheduled time.
- Partial containers are consolidated at the airport and loaded onto the airplane.
- Airplane transports the package to the national hub in Memphis or to a regional hub.
- Containers are unloaded, sorted, and reloaded into containers for the destination city.
- Containers are loaded onto the airplane flying to the destination city.
- Containers are unloaded at the destination airport. An airport in large cities serves many stations in the city and surrounding areas. The airport ramp operation has to sort the

mixed containers before trucking the packages to the respective city stations.

- Trucks are unloaded on the sort belt in the city station and packages are sorted by delivery route.
- Delivery courier drives to the customer location for delivery before the promised service commitment.

Most of these operations take place during the night in a tightly controlled time window. There are occasions when planes are being loaded and unloaded in thunderstorms or snow. For smaller markets, too far to reach by truck from the city airport, there are additional flights on smaller airplanes to and from the city airport. If it is an international package, there are additional steps to go through including customs clearance at both the origin and the destination.

Description of the Hub and Spoke Air Route System

For every purchase, customers want the best value for their dollars whether it is the best service or a quality product at a low price. The same is true for shippers using express transportation for guaranteed, on-time delivery at the lowest cost. That means the shipping company must continually evaluate its systems and processes to improve service and reduce costs.

The original idea for Federal Express, outlined in an undergraduate term paper written by Fred Smith for a course at Yale, has been well publicized. The paper pointed out that passenger route systems for shipping air freight were not going to be able to meet the needs of the growing air freight industry. A system needed to be designed specifically for air freight. Further work in developing this concept into a viable business plan resulted in a *hub and spoke* air route system. After loaded with packages picked up during the day, all planes from cities served in the United States would arrive at a national hub during the night. Each inbound plane would carry packages for deliveries in other cities in the system. The lines connecting the two points, origin or destination city and the national hub, represent the spokes. The beauty of this system is that the hub connects each point in the system with every other point. The packages are sorted and consolidated by destination. The airplanes arrive back in the morning at the city airport with packages from around the country destined for delivery in that city.

It may seem strange for a package going from Chicago to Louisville to go through the national hub in Memphis instead of flying directly to the destination. But it makes financial sense. Airplanes are expensive and have to be fully utilized to keep the cost of doing business and price for the service reasonable. As the business grew, larger markets needed more than one airplane to handle the outbound and inbound package volume. This growth presented the option of flying the second airplane to another location (hub) closer to the markets served. The Indianapolis regional hub was added to the system in 1987. Since then, the system has been enhanced repeatedly.

The most demanding aspect and the critical resource of the express delivery business is *time*, the finite number of hours between pickup and delivery; express packages picked up in the afternoon must be delivered next morning by 10:30 A.M. Every minute counts. If FedEx does not deliver the package on time today, it is not delivering on the absolutely positively overnight promise. If the demand suddenly goes up, the company still has the same number of hours to sort at the origin city, fly to the hub, sort at the hub, fly to the destination city, sort at destination, and deliver. Every function must operate under a tight schedule. The planes have to depart and arrive on time because one late arrival can delay the entire sort at the hub. And a late sort at the hub adversely impacts the whole system the following morning. A glitch in the system may cause 40,000 couriers to be late leaving their stations in the morning to begin the delivery cycle. They still must complete all express deliveries by 10:30 A.M. If the deliveries are not made by 10:30 A.M., the customers can and do exercise a money-back guarantee. It was once estimated that a one-minute delay in the system costs FedEx $1 million.

On the one hand, the operational areas must have predictable processes to produce the desired results day in and day out. At the same time, they have to be flexible enough to handle the increased volume on a given day. Employees in Operations Planning and Engineering at the corporate and regional levels must continually develop plans to increase capacity and operational efficiency for keeping up with double-digit growth rates. Along with running the system on time, operations managers and their employees play a key role: They are responsible for the successful implementation of these plans.

Senior Management's Role in the Innovation Journey

In an innovation economy—where companies can win big just by outthinking the competition—the words "what if we . . . ?" may be the most important phrase in business. But what does it take to come up with an idea? Why can some people and some organizations generate a seemingly endless supply, whereas others struggle to find any idea that is fresh, creative, or out of the ordinary? The answer is that organizations with lots of creative ideas have a thriving innovation culture that engages leaders at all levels in "Leading for Innovation" behaviors: This environment is the key to generating and sharing ideas. Another important feature is having defined processes for each of the three steps for innovation—generating, accepting and evaluating, and implementing the approved ideas. Like any process, they are only as effective as the support they receive from those in leadership positions. Leaders need to be personally involved in facilitating each of these steps.

FedEx had well-defined processes for generating, accepting, and implementing what ifs both at the corporate level and at the operating division levels. Generating ideas at the corporate level was what I did for nine years. The Operations Research department and my department spent the majority of our time thinking about strategic what ifs. The free flow of ideas would start with a note from Fred Smith asking, "What if—to accommodate growth and/or improve service levels—we look at opening up a hub in Dallas/Fort Worth or Greensboro or Paris?" or "What if we make this change in our aircraft fleet?" or "What if we schedule a flight into Bombay?" Other times, a product manager in marketing might think out loud, "What if we introduce this new product?" Or a sales executive would think out loud, "What if we move the cutoff time for picking up packages in certain West Coast zip codes from 4 P.M. to 5 P.M.? That way, we can pick up quite a bit more business." It was not unusual for us to work on four or five "what-if" scenarios at the same time.

Involving All Stakeholders

Each of these changes would have a big impact on the entire organization. So it was important that people from all areas affected by a decision participate in evaluating and developing these ideas. To ensure this, we had three separate meetings per month, scheduled well in advance, to involve people at all levels of the organization. In the first week of the month, the participants were managers and directors. In the second week of the month, the directors and vice presidents met. In the third week of the month, the attendees were the CEO, the senior officers, and the planning directors. The meetings were known throughout the company as LRPC (Long Range Planning Committee) meetings, and everyone was well aware of their strategic importance.

At the manager-level meeting, each manager was expected to share what ifs from his or her area as part of the acceptance and development of the larger idea. These operational what ifs would be discussed in the next meeting at the vice president level. We had freedom to add these generated ideas to the LRPC agenda. After listening to our evaluations, Fred Smith and the senior officers would share their insights. Based on my more than 25 years' experience working and consulting with senior executives, I can vouch that Smith and his team had the rare combination of being visionary strategists, generating idea after idea while understanding the tactics that would be needed for implementation throughout the operation. They took personal interest, provided support, and followed up regularly to guarantee successful execution of the approved plans. This process ensured that all creative options were generated, shared, and evaluated.

Another major responsibility of the Operations Research and System Form Engineering departments was to develop long-range facility plans for all locations around the world. The long-range operations and facilities planning process would start with the Marketing department's release of the three- and five-year business forecasts. Our role was to develop the functional specifications for sorting hubs and other facilities worldwide and to develop and evaluate more efficient operating scenarios for handling increased business volume.

After the operating scenarios, what if evaluations were done, and the long-range facilities plans were ready for presentation to the LRPC. Fred Smith did not want planners and engineers to undertake that task. Instead, he wanted the regional vice presidents to present the final report. His objective was to make sure that the regional management understood and approved the plans. The planners and engineers worked closely with the regional vice presidents to help them prepare for this meeting. After the plans were presented, the last questions Fred would ask were always, "How can I help you implement these plans?" and, "What do you need from me?" He would make a point of following up on the requests made to him.

Notable Innovations

Today, the word FedEx is not just the company's name—it is a verb that people use when they want something delivered to them quickly and on time. People say, "FedEx it to me" in dozens of languages in more than 200 countries throughout the world. So how did this company grow from an unknown start-up to become one of the world's most recognized and trusted brands? Here are some of the innovations that helped make this happen. All of them were driven by market and customer needs.

First Express Shipping Company to Own and Operate Aircrafts, Package-Sorting Facilities, and Delivery Vans (1973)

Customers wanted overnight, reliable, door-to-door service. By controlling all aspects of the operation and the package from pickup to delivery, FedEx could ensure reliable and on-time delivery.

First Air Freight Company to Use Television Advertising (1975)

Express package delivery is both capital and labor intensive. It requires a huge amount of capital to get started. Before FedEx could hang the "Open for Business" sign, there had to be significant investments in airplanes, delivery vans, city stations, and airport sorting facilities. A substantial workforce was needed to pick up, sort, and deliver packages. After buying the airplanes, setting up the support infrastructure, and hiring the employees, the challenge facing FedEx was to spread the word quickly and generate the needed business volume. FedEx Marketing concluded that TV commercials would be the fastest way to make people aware of this new overnight delivery company. This was a bold move for the times as it was unheard of for air freight companies to advertise on TV.

The strategy behind the TV campaign was to create "top-of-the-mind awareness" in customers when they were in need of an express delivery company. The first ads simply said, "America, You've Got a New Airline." These were followed by "Federal Express, When It Absolutely Positively Has to Be There Overnight." The successive ads made excellent use of humor in conveying the message. Within a span of four years, this innovative campaign helped Federal Express become a market leader. These ads were aired more than 25 years ago. But people who saw them can still fondly recall them.

One of the most memorable ads was the "fast-talking man." Actor John Moschitta played the role of a fast-talking, extremely busy executive. He is sitting at his desk, talking on the phone, issuing orders, and making deals at a furious pace. In the background, his assistant is working frantically, trying to keep up with John. In the final scenes, the assistant falls hopelessly behind, and the papers from the copier are flying all over the floor. The fast-talking man needed a fast delivery company to handle his business needs. This ad ends with the following message. "Federal Express now schedules delivery by 10:30 A.M. It's incredible what you can do with that much extra time." Another commercial starring John, in his fast-talking and non-stop business deals making role, ends with "In this fast moving high pressure, get it done yesterday world, aren't you glad that there is one company that can keep up with it all? FedEx, when it absolutely positively has to be there overnight."

Leadership Role in Deregulation of the Air Cargo Industry (1977)

Once customers realized they could ship packages reliably overnight, they wanted to send bigger and heavier shipments. Many cities that were not served by FedEx at that time also wanted overnight service. Both the passenger and cargo airlines were regulated by the Civil Aviation Board (CAB). Until the 1977 air cargo deregulation bill was approved in Congress, the CAB limit for payload capacity for air cargo was 7,500 pounds. This only allowed usage of very small aircrafts such as Falcon jets. By comparison, a 727 (a small aircraft in the passenger airline business) could carry a payload of 40,000 pounds. FedEx, along with all the stakeholders— customers, employees, and chambers of commerce from the cities that wanted overnight service actively worked together in getting this bill passed.

Launched COSMOS (Customers, Operations and Service Master Online System, 1979)

Putting all package-related information in a central computerized system allowed customer service agents to answer customers' queries about the status of their packages. It also allowed operations managers to plan better by having historical as well as current data at their fingertips.

First Express Company to Install Electronic Communication System in Delivery Vans (DADS, Digitally Assisted Dispatch System, 1980)

This innovation allowed couriers to receive on-call pickup requests on a display monitor in their vans. With this information, received on a timely basis, couriers were able to respond to customers' requests immediately. It also eliminated missed pickups.

First Company to Introduce Packaging Materials to Meet Specific Customer Needs—Overnight Letter (1981)

The objective was to make it as easy as possible for customers to do business with FedEx. The fixed price up to a certain weight for any destination was another desirable feature. It also made the sender's package stand out in the recipient's stack of inbound mail and conveyed that it was an important and urgent piece of mail.

First Express Company to Offer Delivery at 10:30 A.M. (1982)

Competitors were offering noon or later deliveries. Customers indicated that they would like to receive their express shipments as early as possible so they would have the full working day to make use of the material or respond to critical correspondence.

First Express Company to Introduce a PC-Based Automated Shipping System (1984)

Customers wanted to speed up the shipping process by eliminating the time spent filling out paperwork. Since then, this system has continually been upgraded and offers customized functions to suit the needs of the shipper.

Introduced SuperTracker, a Hand-Held Bar Code Scanner System (1986)

This is used for scanning the package at each step to track and report package status on real-time basis (see discussion in Chapter 1).

Development of an Integrated, Seamless International and Domestic Network (1989)

In the 1970s and 1980s, more and more goods began moving across borders and the vast oceans separating continents. The manufacture of high-value goods such as chips and other components for the rapidly growing personal computer industry was moving to China and other Asian countries. Memory chips were manufactured in Singapore, hard drives in China, monitors in Malaysia. All of them were transported to the United States for assembly and delivery to U.S. customers.

Anticipating this growth in global trade, FedEx's executive management envisioned an integrated, seamless international and domestic network. The biggest challenge in establishing this network was securing the landing rights at major international airports. To start from scratch would have taken years because landing slots at these extremely busy international airports were hard to come by. Additionally, the approvals for new slots were governed by bilateral government negotiations and regulations, lengthy and involved processes. Starting from scratch would have taken years because of limited availability of landing slots at these extremely busy airports. The innovative strategy of acquiring Flying Tigers helped FedEx obtain these valuable landing rights in one fell swoop.

Flying Tigers was a Los Angeles based freight company that had already acquired landing rights at major airports. Its customers were mainly freight forwarders who offered airport-to-airport service. FedEx's goal was to offer time-definite door-to-door service between U.S. cities and major international destinations.

Not only do international shipments have to go through the usual routine at their origin and destination, they also have to clear customs on both ends. It took innovative thinking in all areas of the company (Strategy, Systems Planning, Scheduling, Engineering, International Operations, and Domestic Operations to name a few) to integrate the international network with the existing domestic network. This integrated, seamless network established a much higher standard of service in the international arena just as the domestic network had done earlier for the U.S. market.

First Service Company to Win the Prestigious Malcolm Baldrige National Quality Award (1990)

This award evaluates all the internal processes to make sure they are focused on providing quality customer service. It also takes into account that all employees are involved in continually improving these processes and level of customer service.

First Company to Offer Online Tracking (1994)

A key innovation for helping customers better manage their business processes came in the form of fedex.com — the first web-based application to offer real-time information on package status. The web site has been continually enhanced to allow customers to do their shipping online, whether domestic or international. It has been selected as the best transportation web site.

Improving Asset Utilization and System Efficiency to Keep Costs Low (1997)

In the 1997 fiscal year, FedEx handled close to 2.5 million domestic packages and over 220,000 international packages. Domestic revenue had grown to $8 billion and international revenue had grown to $3 billion. The growth placed enormous demands on the system and operations. The national hub played an even bigger role in running the system on time to maintain high service levels. To ensure that the national hub in Memphis completed its sort on time, the flights' arrivals were continually evaluated and adjusted. In one such initiative, several flights from North and South Carolina were rescheduled to leave 5 to10 minutes earlier, which had a significant effect on the field operations. Mike Moss, District Director of Field Operations, met with all affected employees to explain why the time would be moved up. He told them that he understood the hardship the initiative would create and that significant changes would have to be made. But, he added that it would help improve FedEx's level of customer service both nationally and globally.

He asked the employees to get together to decide what changes were needed in operations to meet the new flight schedule: How would this change affect customers? How could they reroute the pickup times so couriers could get back into the station earlier? In two days, employees and managers came up with an innovative plan that accommodated the change without any increase in cost or negative impact on the customers. Since they were involved in the plan's development, the employees' commitment for successful implementation was built into it. Mike explained his philosophy to me as follows, "I continually tell the couriers and other station employees that they're the most important players in this operation. I involve each one of them in problem solving and developing implementation plans. If you as manager or director do all the thinking and problem solving, then the only thing you get is what you think. Employees will simply do what they are told and not do any creative thinking. And, FedEx will miss out on employees' creative ideas."

FedEx Express, FedEx Ground, FedEx Freight, FedEx Kinko's

In the business world logistics have become a key factor in gaining a competitive edge. Logistics no longer means just moving goods from point A to point B such as a retailer moving products from the warehouse to the store or a manufacturing company moving spare parts from suppliers to its plants for assembly. The entire logistics design is an integral part of business strategy development and execution. Therefore, customers are looking not just for a shipping company, but a strategic partner who understands their business strategies and works with them to design a logistics solution that helps them gain a competitive edge.

This can and does include using several modes of transportation. To offer comprehensive and complete logistics solutions, FedEx developed and executed a strategy of acquiring companies offering ground and freight services. They were all successfully rebranded under the trusted FedEx brand. To meet the unique demands of Internet retailers it created a Home Delivery service. To accommodate the needs of dual career households, the Home Delivery service offered the option of scheduling deliveries at a time convenient to the customer.

Teamed with Amazon.com to Meet the Needs of an Unprecedented Sales Phenomenon (2000)

The marketing strategy for the much anticipated book *Harry Potter and the Goblet of Fire* called for release of the book nationally on the same day. Amazon.com had taken orders for 250,000 books all to be delivered on the day of its release. Using resources from its various operating companies, FedEx designed and delivered a customized solution for successfully meeting this challenge. In 2003, FedEx followed this feat with the delivery of 400,000 copies of *Harry Potter and the Order of the Phoenix* in a single day, making lots of young readers around the country very happy.

Alliance with U.S. Postal Service to Place FedEx Drop Boxes at Post Offices Nationwide (2001)

The U.S. Postal service (USPS) was looking for reliable air transportation for part of its mail service. This public-private alliance benefited USPS by having reliable air transportation that served its customers, and FedEx was able to make it more convenient for its customers to drop FedEx packages. The innovative part of this alliance is the mind shift of both parties from thinking of themselves as competitors to seeing each other as alliance partners.

An Innovation Continuum

Some of the innovations at FedEx have been major breakthroughs, whereas others have enhanced the existing product or processes. Typically when people talk of innovation, they think of a new technology, product, or service. As Figure 2.1 shows, innovation in the business world is a continuum, from *innovation* to *Innovation*. The *i* changes are the day-to-day thoughts and ideas that can ultimately trigger groundbreaking, earth-shattering *I* ideas that change the world or at the very least, a company.

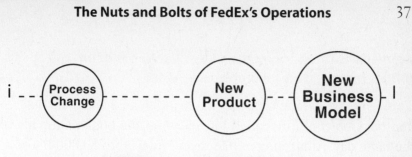

FIGURE 2.1   Innovation Continuum

i: Continuous improvements, small- and midsize changes in business processes leading to improved customer experience, better customer value proposition design (product enhancements), better customer value proposition delivery, improved operational efficiency, and so on.

I: Business model changes, large-scale alterations in the form of disruptive technology, creative use of existing technology to develop new products or services, global expansion, and so on.

Even a business started with a unique ("I") business model needs small- and midscale ("i") changes, or continuous improvement, to sustain its competitive advantage.

Small and Midscale *i* in Support of the Big *I* Business Model

In 1983, 10 years after its start with an innovative business model, FedEx had a highly successful domestic business that had reached $1 billion in sales. FedEx then made international expansion a strategic business priority calling for aggressive expansion in as many countries as possible. From customers' standpoint, having a global network was critical.

Arun Kulkarni was manager of the international expansion department with a staff of five professionals. The charter for his team was coming up with an optimal model that could be replicated for establishing FedEx's presence in different countries. The number one objective for this model was to make sure that operations in each country looked and felt like FedEx. The other objectives were to grow the operation as dictated by business growth and minimization of financial investment at the start. Every country presented unique challenges in terms of regulatory environment, customs clearance, and so on.

I asked Arun the secret behind his team's success in building the network and expanding FedEx's international coverage. He summarized the keys to his team's successful execution of the growth strategy as follows:

1. Creativity of staff in coming up with innovative ideas for adapting the basic model to suit the unique environment of each country.
2. A close, collaborative relationship among his staff and the key players in Legal, Finance, and Marketing.
3. Direct access to and guidance from executive management.
4. Direct access to and close working relationship with officers in FedEx's international regions.
5. Being able to feel and see that we were making a difference.

International business is now the fastest growing segment of the express business with a growth rate in the double digits. The initial idea of expanding the business model to include a fully integrated global network was Innovation. At that time, other shipping companies were offering express international document service. Passenger airlines were offering international air freight and container services. A reliable door-to-door international express package service did not exist. To successfully execute international vision and strategy required hundreds of *i*nnovations at all levels and every facet of the operation.

MARKET- AND CUSTOMER-DRIVEN INNOVATION

The two parts of a successful innovation journey are (1) understanding where a business is on that journey and identifying the root causes (obstacles) that are preventing it from building and sustaining an innovation culture; and (2) developing and implementing an action plan to address the identified root causes.

FedEx's business strategy has been driven by market and customer needs even if it has meant diluting its own business. Overnight express service for delivery by 10:30 A.M. next business morning was growing at a healthy double-digit rate. Customers expressed a need for more economical overnight service. FedEx introduced Standard Overnight for delivery by next business afternoon at a lower price. No doubt, some next-business-morning customers switched to the more economical afternoon delivery. But overall, it brought in more customers and package volume than the company lost from dilution.

Later when market and customers wanted FedEx to offer a complete portfolio of services including the cheaper, day-definite ground service, there was a risk of diluting its own higher revenue express shipments. FedEx pursued the innovative business strategy of developing total business solutions to meet customers' needs for documents, boxes, freight—domestic and international—by combining air and ground transportation services.

Anticipating the changes in the business environment, FedEx decided that it would be better to shift packages from express to ground within the FedEx family than to have the competition do it. (In September 2004, Wonder, the well-known brand in breads, filed for bankruptcy. One reason it was forced to take this action is that it had been slow in responding to the shift in consumer preferences for "low-carb" products.)

The prerequisite for successfully building and sustaining an innovation culture is understanding what has been holding the organization back. What has kept the company from developing and unleashing its natural creative potential? Chapter 3 explores the common root causes behind the lack of a thriving innovation culture in organizations.

Chapter 3

Why Organizations Do Not Innovate

Innovative Thinking? We don't even have time for bad thinking. Innovation. You tell yourself it's a top priority, but between e-mail, meetings and fending off the crisis du jour, you never get to it.

—IBM Ad in *Fortune* magazine, August 9, 2004

"Innovate, innovate, innovate" is the mantra regularly chanted by senior executives. Why then, do so few executives succeed in building and sustaining an innovation culture? There is good news. Every company has the necessary creative resource in abundance: People.

People want to feel that they are making a difference. They want to feel that their work matters. They want to make creative contributions. They want their companies to succeed and to grow, so they, too, will have opportunities for personal and professional growth.

Dr. Joseph Juran is known as the "father of quality management." For over 70 years, he has been helping organizations around the world enhance their competitiveness. He is recognized as the person who added the human dimension to quality:

I can say that those of us who have been around a long time have never seen a limit to human ingenuity. Toyota makes over a million improvements a year. Human beings have no limit to their creativity. The problem is to make it possible for them to use that creativity.

—A conversation with Joseph Juran by
Thomas A. Stewart, *Fortune*, January 11, 1999

All humans have a basic need to express themselves and to develop their natural creative potential. People have a need to self-actualize, or to feel that they are exercising a unique and precious combination of skills and abilities; that they are fulfilling a special purpose or making a special contribution, and that their lives are connected to a larger sense of purpose or meaning. These human needs mesh perfectly with the need for organizations to innovate, as shown in Figure 3.1.

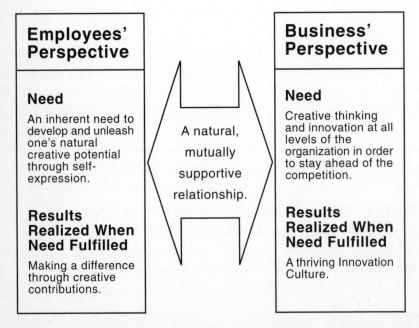

FIGURE 3.1   Mutually Supportive Needs of Employees and Organizations for Creativity and Innovation

Since individuals and organizations have such mutually supportive needs, why isn't there a thriving innovation culture in every organization? During my tenure at FedEx's Leadership Institute, I hosted representatives from several companies who were there to benchmark with FedEx. One of the companies was a Fortune 500 manufacturing firm stuck at zero growth. The company had experienced declining profit margins for several years. In my conversations with the representatives from this company, they acknowledged the key role that employees should play in developing new solutions for customers' changing needs and improving processes to reduce the cost of doing business. During one discussion, the vice president of human resources for this company commented that its executive management team had only recently acknowledged that employees play a role in making money. Up until then, the company had held the belief that machines, or labor, made money. With this type of thinking (viewing employees as pairs of hands versus viewing them as the source of ideas), human resources was left to fight an uphill battle. How could they convince the powers that be that managers should be expected to develop and tap into employees' creative potential?

Through my research and experience, I have identified five root causes that explain the disparities between the desire for innovation and the realities of the business world.

ROOT CAUSE 1: LACK OF SUPPORTIVE LEADERSHIP PRACTICES AND ORGANIZATIONAL PROCESSES

When working with organizations to build an innovation culture, it is essential to talk with employees and managers at different levels. One way to start the process is by forming four small groups of select employees and managers and asking each group to answer one of the following four questions:

Group 1: Why should you worry about innovation?

Group 2: What would innovation look like in your areas of responsibility?

Group 3: How do you create an environment that promotes innovative thinking at all levels of the organization?

Group 4: What stops you from developing and unleashing your creative potential?

The responses to the question for Group 4 almost typically reveal that leadership practices have prevented employees from engaging in innovative thinking and creative problem solving. These unhelpful practices and negative support systems include:

- Discouraging change
- Not being open to looking at different ways of doing things
- Micromanaging
- Resisting challenges by employees
- Bureaucratic systems that slow things down
- Indecisive management
- Lack of time for creative thinking due to busy schedules
- Turf protections as a result of departmental isolation and lack of collaboration or cross-pollination between departments
- Lack of challenging goals and direction
- Inability of managers to discuss conflicting ideas on a professional level
- Close-minded managers who are not willing to listen to new ideas
- A culture that suggests to get ahead one must not make waves and must play politically safe
- Fear of failure

The majority of managers can describe the desirable leadership behaviors that will inspire employees to develop and unleash their creative potential. So why is there such a large gap between intellectual understanding of the right leadership practices and their application on the job? First, there is a lack of understanding that three equally important skill sets—technical, managerial, and leadership—are all required for successful outcomes.

Second, there is a lack of awareness that effective leadership is the result of a distinct skill set and is more an affair of the heart (right-brain) than the head (left-brain). Psychological research has shown that the left side of the brain controls segmented, analytical, and rational processes. The right side supports conceptual, creative, and feeling processes. The analytical side makes for good planners, organizers, and controllers—and thus, effective *managers*. The feeling and conceptual side makes for visionary, caring, and inspiring managers—and thus effective *leaders*.

Finally, there is a lack of insight into factors influencing human behaviors and motivation. People in the management ranks and leadership positions who come with a technical, engineering, finance, accounting, or information systems background are programmed with a strong preference for analytical and rational activities. Traditional leadership training does not address this reality.

Robin Robinson, a human resource consultant with extensive experience in the business world agreed with this perception. "I saw what you are saying in real-time. It seems that technical managers were not taught how to lead others during college. Everything is either black or white; it works or it won't work. There are no gray areas in their line of work—kind of like math, one plus one equals two and nothing else," she said. "That causes a real challenge to lead, to create a synergistic team, inspire creativity, and welcome other approaches to solving problems."

Following are three reasons some technically proficient managers are not inspiring leaders.

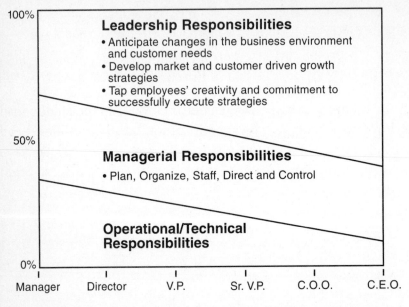

FIGURE 3.2 Three Skill Sets for Adding Full Value as a Manager

1. *Lack of understanding that three equally important skill sets— technical, managerial, and leadership—are necessary to add maximum value.*

Managers have three distinct sets of responsibilities that call for three distinct skills sets. As one moves up in the organization, the successful fulfillment of leadership responsibilities adds the most value. As the responsibility diagram (see Figure 3.2) and the research by author James Cribbin show, effective leadership is the key for getting the maximum effort from employees.

Supported by authority and regulations, you can get people to work 60 to 65 percent capacity—just enough to satisfy minimum job requirements. Leadership is a multiplier factor that deals with the other 35 to 40 percent. A mere administrator can achieve average results. The leader gets superior results from average people. Management is largely an action-oriented cerebral process. Leadership is an action-oriented interpersonal process.

—James J. Cribbin, Leadership Strategies for Organizational Effectiveness, AMACOM, New York

As Figure 3.2 shows, when a person moves up the ladder, leadership duties become a bigger part of total responsibilities. Leading a greater number of people means that leadership skills play a key role in tapping creativity and commitment of this large employee base.

2. *Lack of awareness that leadership is a completely distinct skill set, more an affair of the heart (feeling) than the head (analysis).*

Being an effective leader means influencing and encouraging employees to give the gift of their discretionary effort—their creativity and commitment. This is how organizations can ensure that they are designing and delivering products and services that are superior to those of the competition.

An employee gives this gift of commitment when the leader through day-to-day behaviors makes the employee *feel*:

- I am part of a winning team that is going somewhere.
- I am making a difference.
- The leader cares about me as a person:
  - I am supported in my life beyond work.
  - I am challenged and growing professionally.
  - I am appreciated when I go above and beyond.
  - I am listened to when I have ideas to share.

The key word in understanding the leadership process is *feel*.

When managers spend the majority of their time analyzing productivity, sales goals, and budget numbers, they often ignore the inspiring (feeling) side of leading people. This tends to make them inaccessible because people relate to and connect with others at the feeling level. Feelings play both a positive and a negative role in job performance and in motivating and engaging employees. Feelings of security, optimism, appreciation, and mutual trust boost energy, creativity, and initiative. Feelings of insecurity, pessimism, lack of appreciation, and trust block energy, creativity, and initiative.

3. *Lack of insight into factors influencing human behaviors and motivation.*

"Why is he behaving this way?" It is a familiar question. To understand the visible behavior, we need to understand some of the invisible factors operating in the background. What the person knows, how he feels, and how supportive he finds environment play a major role in answering the question. A person may know how to do the job, but if he feels disengaged, he is not going to go out of his way to solve problems. A person may have an innovative idea, but will not pursue it if risk is discouraged, success is not rewarded, and failure is punished. Harry Levinson summed up the central role feelings play at work and how difficult it is for so many managers to deal with them in his review of Manfred F. R. Kets de Vries's book, *Life and Death in the Executive Fast Lane*:

> Is management in reality a rational task performed by rational people according to sensible organizational objectives? We all know better, yet the myth of rationality persists in spite of all evidence to the contrary. Much of our society and most of our business life is organized around airtight logic, numbers, and explanations that "make sense." However, a whole range of logic-defying emotions—rage, fear, insecurity, jealousy, and passion—is acted out in the office. It is these powerful yet unacknowledged feelings that often disrupt our organization.
>
> Most executives have a notoriously underdeveloped capacity for understanding and dealing with emotions. All but the

best are reluctant to ask themselves why they act the way they do. As a result, most fail to understand both their own managerial behavior and that of others.

—Harry Levinson, *Harvard Business Review*, review of
the book, *Life and Death in the Executive Fast Lane*,
by Manfred F. R. Kets de Vries, January/February 1996

ROOT CAUSE 2: LACK OF UNDERSTANDING THAT INNOVATION IS IMPERATIVE

Although CEOs say that they understand the need for innovation because of the ever-changing business environment, at lower management levels, there is still resistance and a belief that new ideas are an option instead of a necessity. In both boom times and hard times, companies are unwilling to make the leap to innovation. If the company is doing well, the attitude is, "We are doing well. It's tough enough to keep up with the growth." This attitude fosters complacency. If people are spending all of their time and energy on current business and internal operational issues, they cannot look ahead and see the big picture (changing demographics, technical developments, and customer needs).

If a company is not doing well, the attitude is, "We were growing before the economic slowdown and will grow again as soon as the economy picks up. We just need to cut expenses to survive and maintain our profitability during this no-growth period." But as history has demonstrated, companies cannot cut, outsource, or downsize their way to economic success. They have to grow. This was true 100 years ago, 20 years ago, and even more so in today's fast-changing global economy.

The preference for sticking with the status quo, fear of the unknown, and management's belief that innovation is an option are attitudes that trickle down to employees, who also adopt that way of thinking.

Managers generally understand that the marketplace is always changing and the company must change accordingly to stay in business and grow. They will say things are changing and cite examples of recent changes they have implemented. But what is missing from this understanding is that to grow a company's internal rate of change (e.g., new business strategy, business processes, products, and distribution systems that are controlled by the company) must be higher than the external rate of change (changes that are outside the control of the company). If the external rate of change exceeds the internal rate, a company will lose its competitive edge and market share.

The arrows in Figure 3.3 represent the squeeze put on companies by the rate of change in the larger business environment (external changes) where competition occurs. The only way to neutralize this external pressure and gain market share is to counter it with a higher internal rate of change.

The first step in gaining market share is to understand the changes taking place in the larger business environment. The second step is to engage the enterprise in developing innovative solutions that capitalize on the opportunities presented by the changes.

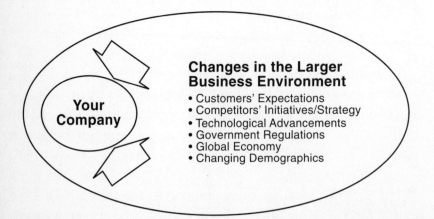

FIGURE 3.3   Gaining Market Share in the Changing Business Environment

In today's fast-changing business environment, the speed in developing and implementing innovative solutions is the key to staying ahead of the competition.

Motorola was slow in moving to digital technology in its cellular phones and as result lost its market leadership position to competitors. Similarly, Xerox was slow in understanding and adapting to technological changes. As a result, it lost a significant share of the market. As discussed in Chapter 2, FedEx has maintained its leadership position and market share by continually developing and implementing innovative business strategy, processes, and products.

Balancing Predictability and Change

Organizations have two paradoxical needs to grow and stay ahead of the competition. They need predictable processes to deliver consistent quality. At the same time, they need new ideas that will disrupt those existing processes and products. People have similar conflicting needs. We need to take risks to grow, but we also need stability and predictability for peace of mind. Gary Hamel, a best-selling author and chairman of Strategos, a strategy-consulting firm, has made similar observations in his work developing business strategies for global organizations:

> Innovation, experimentation, and creativity are tolerated, when safely corralled in R&D or product-development units, or locked up inside of incubators and new venture divisions, but they are seldom full-throated rivals to optimization and incrementalism. Put simply, most companies don't do paradox well.
>
> This lopsided enthusiasm was perhaps forgivable in a world where change meandered rather than lurched. But in a discontinuous world, inability to manage the paradox of optimization and innovation amounts to a mortal sin. To thrive in turbulent

times, a company must do more than retrench: It must give customers new and compelling reasons to spend; it must reinvent
its cost structure; it must build new growth platforms that leverage its competencies and assets. All that takes innovation.

> —Gary Hamel, "The American Paradox,"
> *Fortune*, November 12, 2001

Another factor contributes to leaders' failure at encouraging
and expecting innovation as a matter of course. Too often, they are
internally focused—fully occupied with what is happening inside
the organization. There is no process or expectation to keep up
with the changes in the larger business environment that they compete in—the external world:

> Our challenge was not that we had lost the timeless assets that
> once made us great. The problem was that we had become too
> inwardly focused. We were too busy celebrating our great past
> and no longer searching for our future. We were operating as a
> company of independent silos and not a coherent collective.

> —Carly Fiorina, CEO, HP, *Silicon India*, August 2001

A misconception leaders have is that the engineers in research
laboratories are the only ones responsible for innovations. But the
reality is that everyone in the organization should be involved in
designing and/or delivering value to its customers. Therefore, every
employee must be involved in the innovation process to enhance
an organization's competitive edge.

ROOT CAUSE 3: LACK OF COLLABORATIVE THINKING ACROSS DEPARTMENTS AND DISCIPLINES

The president of an international company invited me to evaluate
the extent of innovative thinking in his organization. I had long

conversations with each of the department heads to help me understand how they and their organization valued innovation.

Each person I interviewed said that the company could grow much faster and improve profitability if there were better alignments between departments—between design and manufacturing, marketing and design, manufacturing and logistics, and so on. This cross-pollination of disciplines has been proven time and time again across industries to breed innovation as people from different backgrounds and with different approaches work together to solve common problems. By failing to encourage such collaboration the company was missing valuable opportunities to come up with innovations that could increase its market share.

Innovation spurs not only the creation of new products, but also new approaches to old products and services. I have worked with numerous organizations that identified huge revenue growth potential from the selling of one business unit's products and services to the customers of another and vice versa. Successful execution of this strategy requires businesses to develop seamless business processes across all components.

Joining Forces to Satisfy Customer Needs

Marco Chan, an operations director for FedEx, joined the Leadership Institute at the same time I did. He had worked in New Orleans, Beijing, Singapore, and other cities around the world. One example of collaboration from his time in New Orleans demonstrates this point beautifully.

Because of a significant growth in convention business in New Orleans, FedEx saw an increase in shipments of equipment and supplies coming into New Orleans. Packages for the conventions arrived on Fridays. After the conventions were over, the packages were shipped out of New Orleans on Mondays.

This surge in the inbound volume on Fridays created big problems for operations. The operating scenario for all stations was set up so that stations received containers of all their packages on the Friday morning flight from the national hub. The packages were unloaded on the sort belt where couriers would pick off the ones destined for delivery on their route. Because of the high package volume on Fridays, the sorting belts became clogged. Couriers were delayed leaving the building and struggled to make all the morning deliveries on time.

Marco, who was managing director of district operations, along with his operations manager and a sales executive, flew to Memphis for a meeting with their counterparts to collaborate in solving this problem. The group thought out loud, "What if the convention packages were separated from the rest of the New Orleans packages in different containers? And these containers could simply bypass the station completely and be delivered to the convention center directly?"

The operations group in the hub accepted the idea and worked together to implement it. Implementation required collaboration among five departments—Sales (identifying the convention customers), Engineering (working out the logistics), Hub Operations (training the package sorters), New Orleans airport (loading the containers on the trucks), and Station Operations (meeting the truck at the convention center). This solution significantly improved the service levels and reduced costs at the same time.

Public and Private Cooperation

Arun Kumar, Managing Director of FedEx India from 1997 to 1999, shared another example of collaboration. When Arun took charge of the FedEx operations in India, some dutiable shipments took up to 21 days to clear customs—a standard that was not at all acceptable to FedEx. He challenged his management team to reduce the customs clearance window by 50 percent as quickly as possible. In the United States, most packages are cleared by customs the same day. In fact, most are cleared en route because of the detailed information provided by FedEx to the customs department electronically. Three organizations—FedEx, the local transportation company (contracted by FedEx), and the Indian customs department—were involved in the customs clearance process. Having grown up in India and worked at FedEx in the United States, Kumar knew that he could not simply duplicate the process and systems developed in the United States. So he focused on building mutually trusting relationships with the management of the transportation company and customs. A team composed of members from all three organizations examined in detail the entire clearance process, specifically the information required by each organization to preclear and expedite the process. The goal of reducing the time for clearance through customs by 50 percent was achieved within weeks, and the team was given a new goal to reduce the new window by another 50 percent. When Arun left India in 1999, the customs clearance window had been reduced from 21 days to 3 days.

Marco and Arun were not just willing to collaborate, they led the way. This visible participation by leaders led to the development of a model for future collaborative efforts and expectation that their employees would work together. It also reinforced the lesson that small innovative ideas cumulatively can have a huge effect on market share and profitability.

ROOT CAUSE 4: LACK OF BALANCE BETWEEN INNOVATION EXPECTATION AND EMPLOYEES' ABILITY TO DELIVER

When FedEx employees are promoted into the first three levels of management, they are required to attend weeklong leadership development classes at the Leadership Institute at the corporate headquarters in Memphis. Instead of having the human resources department training staff conduct the sessions, the Leadership

Institute recruits some of the best senior managers and managing directors from the company's operating divisions to facilitate the classes.

The thinking behind this approach is that people who have proven to be good leaders have instant credibility in the classroom. They use their experience and expertise to develop new leaders. They can breathe life into the curriculum by relating it to their real-world experiences. By stepping out of management temporarily into this new role, they grow in new directions as they reflect on their own leadership styles. Whenever possible on the last day of the class, Fred Smith, CEO of FedEx, spoke to the classes and engaged in informal conversations with the participants.

During my tenure at the Leadership Institute, I facilitated a class for 16 newly promoted managing directors from all over the world. During our time together, we discussed "Challenging the Process"—the practice of challenging and improving the current processes, the business model, and the status quo with innovative thinking. Throughout the week, there was resistance from the participants, who questioned the reality of this practice. They expressed this sentiment: "It's easy for you to stand in a class and talk about challenging the process. In the real world you get your wrist slapped by management if you try to challenge and change things."

During my session, Fred Smith was in town and available to speak. As we were walking to the classroom, I relayed to him the group's concerns about challenging the process and the feeling that management did not support such initiatives.

He began his talk by explaining the current global business environment and FedEx's growth strategy for competing in the global economy. Midway through his presentation, he paused to tell the group that if they got only one thing from the class, he wanted them to know that the only thing not challenged at FedEx is how the company treats people. Everything else—how it picks up, sorts, and delivers packages; how it processes information; and the customer experience—needed to be continually challenged to make them better. "You have my support for doing that," he told them.

Still they were not convinced and argued that their immediate supervisors were not open to such ideas. Further discussions revealed that many felt overwhelmed because of a lack of balance between the expectations for challenging the process and their abilities—knowledge, skill base, and time to meet all the expectations. In response, I shared with them my personal experiences.

In my 22 years at FedEx, I had found the door of every senior officer open any time I had an idea to share. But there is a trick to it, I told them. Because of demands on management's time, it is important to think out the idea clearly and answer the following questions before approaching the manager:

- What is the opportunity for improving the current business process?
- What is your analysis of the root causes that are stopping us from taking advantage of this opportunity?
- What are your ideas for addressing these root causes?
- And, finally what are the business benefits of making this improvement—order of magnitude only?

Jim Barksdale, FedEx COO in the late 1980s and early 1990s, said repeatedly that if it is not on paper, it is not communicated. But the bigger benefit of answering these questions on paper is that doing so clarifies the thought process.

When I asked them, "How many times in the past year have you approached your boss or other officers with improvement ideas with these questions answered and articulated on paper?" Not a single person raised a hand. This was not a skill that they had developed or used so far in their careers.

Opportunities for Contribution beyond Job Description

Each day of this weeklong class, we had invited a senior officer to speak to the class. The two main objectives for these talks were to introduce the participants to the senior officers, and to help the new managers make contributions at the corporate level.

Tracy Schmidt, Chief Financial Officer, gave one of these talks. He shared with the participants the overall financial and business outlook for the company. He talked about the key roles they play in helping the company develop and successfully execute the business strategy. He said, "You work in the field and are much closer to the action. You know better than us whether the proposed business strategy and the strategic initiatives will work as planned at the operating level. We are looking to you to do the sanity check and advise us." To meet this expectation, he told them—required them—to think at a strategic level, a skill that many had not developed and used before.

Bill Fraine, Senior Vice President of Sales, also spoke to the group. He said, "You play a key role in helping the company meet its sales goals. We are looking to you to closely work with the account executives in calling upon the important customers in your area." Meeting this expectation required making time on their already fully booked calendars.

When feeling overwhelmed mentally (internally), it is a natural human reaction and defense mechanism to find problems externally. These people had just been promoted to managing director positions, very visible and important positions in the company. They were trying to adjust in their new and expanded roles. They were all very driven, proven high performers in their positions as managers before stepping into the managing director roles. They did not like the feeling of not being able to meet the expectations and not feeling on top of everything in this new role.

In too many organizations, people who get promoted to mid and upper level management positions, are pretty much left on their own. There is more training for hourly workers when they are promoted to front-line supervisory positions than for managers promoted into directors and then vice presidential positions. It is very important that organizations allocate the needed resources to help directors and vice presidents develop and unleash their full potential.

Those of us who had been in the director's role for many years at FedEx could relate to their concerns. And we knew from our experience that in due time, and with guidance and coaching from peers and bosses, they would learn the needed skills and become comfortable in their new roles.

ROOT CAUSE 5: LACK OF AN EASILY UNDERSTOOD AND REPLICABLE INNOVATION CULTURE MODEL

Most CEOs and their staffs have heard lectures and presentations on building and sustaining an innovation culture. While the presentations are interesting and sometimes entertaining, one question always remains, "What do I do now?" The need for an innovation culture model has been established in many books, publications, and presentations. But the missing ingredient in the traditional presentations is that the model must be rooted in the understanding of the source of ideas—the human mind. From this new and deeper understanding, companies need a model that outlines how to develop the creative potential in oneself and in others—a model that is easily replicable.

Normally, if a CEO requests a list of "innovative ideas" to include in a report or presentation, employees begin to rack their brains to make a list. In a company with an innovation culture, everyone, as a part of their day-to-day work life, is actively involved in generating, accepting, and implementing ideas. In this environment, there is a ready and growing list of ongoing innovative ideas and projects that regularly and proactively appears on the CEO's and executive managers' desks.

The following chapters present a proven model and practical steps for building and sustaining an innovation culture. The discussion and practical ideas can help managers develop an understanding of not only the necessity of innovation, but also the leadership processes that can make it a part of their corporate cultures. People and organizations have complex well-developed systems aimed at preserving the status quo. The chapters acknowledge this, present ideas for dealing with this reality, and provide managers with the tools to grow an innovation and performance culture that engages every employee in fulfilling the company's goal of increasing its market share and profitability.

Chapter 4

The Five Dimensions of an Innovation and Performance Culture

Throughout its quarter-century history, FedEx has continued to set standards for logistics and transportation services by which all others are judged. This reflects leadership of a high order that promises continued innovation for many years to come.

—Aaron J. Gellman, PhD, Director of the Transportation
Center at Northwestern University, in *How Time Flies*,
a publication celebrating FedEx's 25th anniversary, 1998

Historically, businesses seeking a successful future have relied on discovering the next "big idea"—often an accidental encounter with something great that will carry the company ahead. But to compete successfully and continue to grow in today's ever-changing business environment, companies must learn how to develop a thriving innovation culture—a continuous capacity for generation, acceptance, and implementation of creative ideas—inside the organization, as shown in Figure 4.1.

How does an organization get creative ideas? By continually generating lots of ideas and choosing the ones that address the problem(s) at hand, or that best take advantage of opportunities to fulfill changing customer needs. Where do the ideas come from? Ideas come from our minds. We do not have to make the mind think.

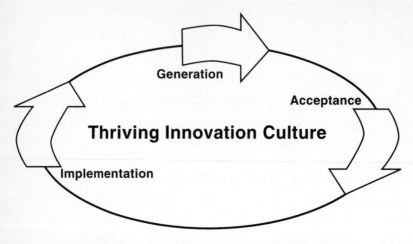

FIGURE 4.1   The Three-Step Innovation Process

That is what nature programmed it to do. However, many people become tense when they are asked for new ideas because the optimum conditions for creative thought are not in place. Who accepts and develops the creative (raw) ideas? The people affected by the idea along with the people who have the knowledge to develop it. Again, acceptance, like generation, is a function of the mind. And the mind readily accepts new ideas when it is functioning under the right conditions. Please note in this chapter, while developing the innovation culture model, often I'll be using the word mind in place of people's mind or people with an objective of making the discussion and understanding of the conditions a little deeper.

CREATIVITY IS ASKING "WHAT IF . . ."

Creativity in the business world involves continuously asking "What if . . . ?" Yet when faced with a problem, people tend to quickly lock into "how to"—a quick solution—before exploring all the options. An easy way to measure the creative environment in an organization is to count how often someone in the company asks questions like "What if we frame the problem this way?" "What if we look at the relationship between these variables?" "What if we explore these options?"

Although the fact seems obvious, most approaches to developing creative potential ignore that ideas are generated in and by the mind. Any manager can tell you that for workers to do their jobs effectively, their environment should be conducive to achieving their tasks. Physical comfort, safety, functional efficiency, and simplicity of design are important components of a good workspace. But there is much more to it than that.

Although physical conditions have some bearing on mental sharpness, other conditions and circumstances are often more important. The challenge is to determine the appropriate design of *mental* space. What conditions facilitate generation, acceptance, and implementation of creative ideas? These conditions increase the probability of creativity becoming a natural part of the problem-solving process. Determining the right mental environment means that leaders must understand first its characteristics and then learn how to affect conditions in that environment. The following story illustrates the importance of the right conditions and underscores two important facts: (1) The people within an organization have vast untapped potential and capabilities; (2) the company's leaders play a critical role in creating the conditions for developing and unleashing employees' potential.

The company was heavily in debt and about to go under. A board meeting was called, after which the chairman, in despair, retired to his office and said, "Lord, I can either get drunk or pray. If I get drunk, I'll feel like hell tomorrow. If I pray, something could happen." He prayed in silence and heard: "Create the conditions within which the individual can develop to his or her greatest capacity within the opportunities at hand." The company recovered and was out of debt in three years.

—A story told by the Reverend Morton T. Kelsey
at a retreat attended by Anne Watson of Marion,
Massachusetts. Submitted by Anne and published in the
March–May 2001 issue of *IONS Noetic Sciences Review*

My experiences with one of the most innovative companies in the history of free enterprise—FedEx—and my success in helping other companies become truly innovative has shown me:

- Everyone has the capacity to be creative.
- Creativity is a function of the mind and must be understood in the context of a mental model.
- Developing creative people (minds) requires the right mental environment (model) and the right leadership practices.
- A critical mass of creative people will enable the development of an organization-wide culture of innovation.

THE INNOVATION CULTURE MODEL

An innovation culture has five dimensions, or conditions. All the conditions must be present for organization-wide creative thinking and innovation. This chapter describes each of the five conditions and explains how they work together to form the ideal model for innovation. It also identifies a manager's day-to-day leadership responsibilities for creating the required conditions.

THE FIRST DIMENSION: ENGAGED PEOPLE

Using colorful PowerPoint slides and flashy presentations, senior managers can present a seemingly convincing case (at least from

FIGURE 4.2 First Dimension of an Innovation and Performance Culture

their standpoint) for why their organization must innovate. After the presentation, employees go back to their workstations and continue to do what they were doing before. Weeks go by and nothing changes because their minds are not engaged in the enterprise. And engagement is essential to generate creative ideas.

When employees' minds become engaged, they focus their mental energies on developing and successfully executing their company's business growth strategies while simultaneously fulfilling their job responsibilities. An engaged mind is fully present and eager to anticipate and understand the changing business environment as well as the opportunities presented by these changes. And the engaged mind taps its natural creative capabilities to develop innovative solutions that take advantage of these new opportunities. When the collective mind of the organization is engaged in the enterprise, the natural by-product is teamwork by employees across departments and disciplines to develop and implement creative ideas that will achieve a common goal (see Figure 4.2).

The Need to Be Part of a Winning Team

So what engages people in the enterprise? Workers' minds become engaged if they feel that they have a stake in what is going on. Employees want to be valued members of a winning team on a mission to make things happen. The leader of that team is responsible for creating a shared vision that engages the employees in the enterprise. But this and other leadership responsibilities usually end up taking a backseat to the pressing day-to-day pressures of meeting productivity and sales goals. Leaders engage people by taking time, on a regular basis, to answer the following questions:

- What is our business *growth* strategy?
- How is our business strategy *relevant* to what I do?
- What, *specifically*, should I do to aid in the growth strategy?
- What's in it for me?

The Need to Make a Difference

There is model of a clipper ship outside the executive management offices at FedEx. Fred used to say that our planes are the clipper ships of the computer age; linking nations together, increasing world trade, and thus helping raise the standard of living for people around the world. FedEx management continually reminds its employees that they are providing critical delivery services—medical supplies for the afflicted, essential spare parts that keep machines and factories running, time-sensitive legal documents, even children's birthday gifts. The company handles and ships all this precious cargo everyday.

To help employees understand where they fit in and how they might benefit from the organization's success, managers need to answer the question, "What's in it for me?" To answer this question, managers must first understand what drives or motivates most employees. Studies have shown that two needs are near the top on the list of what's meaningful to employees:

1. The desire to make a difference
2. The desire to grow professionally and realize their aspirations

Of course, economic factors play an important role. Employees need to earn a decent wage to support themselves and their families. Sharing in the financial success of the company has also proven to be a good motivator. FedEx's profit-sharing plan is an important part of its People First philosophy. Under the right conditions, employees will feel compelled to try to make a difference.

> I didn't help her out because I was looking for a pat on the back. I just did what I could to help a customer in a tough situation. You want to do the right things for people. You want to put yourself in their shoes, as if you were asking for help. Part of customer service is the great feeling that you get when you see that you've made a difference.
>
> —James Briscoe, FedEx Courier, Boston, Massachusetts, *Fast Company*, March 2000

Being fully engaged in the enterprise requires that both the head and the heart are engaged. Engaged employees help the organization achieve its business goals. But employees also want to feel that their work benefits the community-at-large—that there is a greater purpose beyond profit for their work. That is why it is so important for managers to equate the company's mission with a lofty, noble purpose and ensure that employees understand how they fit into the overall scheme of things.

This engagement is achieved by creating excitement and a sense of belonging among employees so that they *feel* they are playing an important role in the organization's success. What is critical to engaging minds is the visible passion of the manager. A leader's emotions are contagious. This enthusiasm and outward show of passion engages the heart.

THE SECOND DIMENSION: GROWING PEOPLE

With the mind engaged, employees are now eager to make contributions to the enterprise. But the generation of new and creative ideas is not as simple as it may seem.

When looking for these creative ideas and innovative solutions, it is often said that one should "think outside the box." But what exactly is this proverbial "box"? You can think of it as the space in the brain that contains all those bits of information and connections made so far. A dot is a bit of information in the knowledge base. And after solving a problem, repeatedly the same way, the connections become automatic. So, when a person is faced with the same problem, the mind, without any conscious effort presents the old, known solution. In many ways, the mind operates like a computer. It scans the knowledge base in the memory (mind) to come up with creative solutions. If the knowledge base is old, the ideas generated may be obsolete. If the knowledge base is limited to a very small part of the total business process or operation, then the solution will only take that area into account.

Solutions that are derived from the same thought processes that the mind has used for years are unlikely to be innovative. The requirement for outside-the-box thinking is the ability to make new connections. New connections can be made in one of two ways; (1) having more dots to connect (a new or updated knowledge base) along with an active imagination, (2) connecting the old dots in new imaginative ways.

Because creativity is the ability to connect seemingly unrelated variables (the dots we store in our minds) in imaginative ways, employees must continually update their knowledge bases to keep up with the fast pace of changing technology (see Figure 4.3).

FIGURE 4.3   Second Dimension of an Innovation and Performance Culture

Operations managers who are familiar only with their own work functions and have no knowledge of the total business process will have limited and incomplete ideas and solutions. They will be unable to evaluate any proposed changes in their departments in terms of the total effect on the rest of the organization. The same thing holds true for keeping up with knowledge in a specific field. Engineers who have been out of school for several years may have been on the cutting edge when they graduated, but they may not have kept up with advances in their field, especially the advancements in technology.

For several years at FedEx, I was a member of the management team responsible for developing long-range global facilities plans for sorting hubs and airport operations worldwide. The planning process—beginning with the marketing department's business forecast and ending with facilities requirements and specifications—at one time took six months. By the time we had our plans ready, the business forecast often had changed. With that concern in mind, the senior vice president of Central Support Services set a goal that we cut the total process time by at least half. We needed to come up with a way to respond to the changing market conditions more rapidly.

We accomplished this objective by expanding the group's knowledge base to include Bill Wilkinson who was an expert in database management and modeling. In addition to automating data from one department to the next, Bill built models to automate the time-consuming number-crunching processes. Bill then trained the facilities planning engineers to use the system. Because of the expanded skill base and new tools, the engineers were able to evaluate more creative operating scenarios. This updated knowledge base not only helped shorten the total process time by more than half, but also vastly improved the work quality and significantly reduced the capital requirements. Adding a new skill set to the team charged with the objective expanded the knowledge base and capabilities of the group as a whole. Additionally, the training and tools provided by Bill helped the engineers expand their individual knowledge and skill base.

Organizations at both the employee and management levels should expect and ensure that the collective knowledge base is updated with internal changes/processes and external advancements. Systems and resources must support this expectation.

Right Brain Thinking: Imagination

Creativity in the business world requires seeing the bigger picture—the connection between seemingly unrelated variables—and putting the pieces together. These creative and intuitive processes rely on the right side of our brain—the imaginative and intuitive side—more than on the analytical left side (see Figure 4.4).

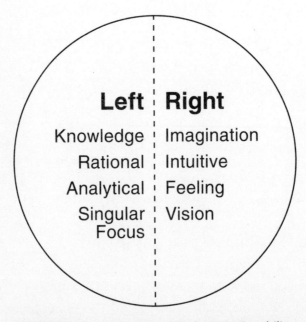

FIGURE 4.4   Imagination: A Right Brain Capability

Einstein said that he never discovered anything with his rational mind and that imagination is more important than knowledge.

When it comes to innovation, the question is not how to innovate but how to invite ideas. How do you invite your brain to encounter thoughts that you might not otherwise encounter? Creative people let their mind wander, and they mix ideas freely. Innovation often comes from unexpected juxtapositions, from connecting subjects that aren't necessarily related. Another way to generate ideas is to treat a problem as though it were generic. If you're experiencing a particular problem, odds are that other people are experiencing it too. Generate a solution, and you may have an innovation.

—Vinton Cerf, with Robert Kahn, devised
TCP/IP (Transmission Control Protocol/Internet
Protocol), a set of standard protocols that
serves as the common language of the Internet,
Fast Company, April 2000

Imagination provides new pathways for neurons to travel and engage in whole brain thinking. Fred Smith came up with the idea of using the hub-and-spoke system for shipping documents and packages because he knew that it was the way the central bank cleared checks. He connected that bit of knowledge with his belief that high-tech industries would need time-definite express transportation. The more knowledge we have, the higher the probability for generating and developing innovative solutions.

THE THIRD DIMENSION: SECURE PEOPLE

The mind is engaged in the enterprise. It has an updated knowledge base—new dots—and using its power of imagination is generating creative ideas. Any creative what-if cannot be fully developed

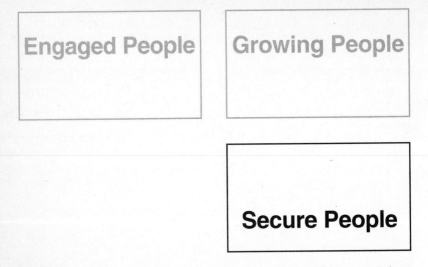

FIGURE 4.5   Third Dimension of an Innovation and Performance Culture

unless the person feels secure internally to voice it, especially in front of the manager and higher-ups. We all have egos, and the higher up we move on the corporate ladder the bigger the ego seems to become. If the proposed idea is different from the manager's own preferred solution, then the manager has to feel secure and ego-free to accept it (see Figure 4.5).

Secure Minds Expressing "What If . . . ?"

An engaged employee with an updated knowledge base attends a meeting, and comes up with a few ideas. But he is insecure about verbalizing them for fear that he will look inadequate in front of his boss and colleagues. So he keeps his potentially great ideas to himself. How do managers draw these ideas out of their subordinates? They must do two things: (1) They must create an environment where employees feel secure to share ideas—both good and bad; and (2) as leaders, they must feel secure about accepting ideas and approaches to solutions that may be different from their own and be willing to accept the risk that comes with change.

The less secure a person feels internally, the greater the need to control things externally. That can often translate into voicing criticism, withholding approval, making all decisions, and creating an "only do things my way" mentality. This behavior weakens the effective leadership needed to create a thriving innovation culture. For a creative idea to become a fully realized innovation, it has to be accepted by both the manager and the people involved in its development.

How does a leader develop the security needed to run an innovation culture? What constitutes security?

Inner security comes from belief in our professional competence, loving relationships, active spiritual life, and a supportive social network. Secure persons can handle the rejection of their ideas at work because they are not dependent on a career as the only source of self-esteem. Development of loving relationships, spiritual life, and supportive social network requires time and energy on a sustained basis. It does not happen overnight or by accident. It requires work/life balance—the allocation of our time and energy to all areas important to us. Admittedly, there is no such thing as a perfect balance. There will be days, weeks, or even months when work may consume most of the waking hours. But if it goes on for years, it takes a toll—physically, mentally, spiritually. And since each individual is at a different place in his or her life journey, what constitutes balance for one person may be completely different from what it means for someone else at a particular stage in life.

Since retiring from FedEx, I have delivered speeches and facilitated seminars on business topics including life balance and building and sustaining successful companies. During these seminars, it was not uncommon for people to say that they really enjoyed their work and did not mind working 16-hour days, 7 days a week. My answer to this sentiment is that building lasting, successful companies requires *long-distance leadership*. Managers and employees in an organization may work 16 hours and be effective in the short run. But, over the long haul, working 16 hours a day will burn people out and will diminish their effectiveness. It is in an organization's best interest to practice and support a work/life balance.

This long-distance leadership theory rang true for a successful Silicon Valley company CEO who heard me speak. He told me that when he started the company, he spent every waking hour on the job. The company was profitable. But, he said, "I'm not having fun and I'm not as creative as I used to be." He was experiencing burnout.

The mind (psyche) has multiple needs that, gone unmet, result in inner conflicts. Leading a balanced life is the only way to meet these needs. A balanced lifestyle that celebrates all of life to its fullest will produce a calm and balanced mind. Unresolved life conflicts do not go away, they just continue to use up a great chunk of our mental energy, reducing the fuel available for our brain to make new connections. The unresolved inner conflicts act as a dam on the flow of creative intelligence.

Secure Minds Accepting Others' Ideas

Once there is tranquility and balance in our lives, the people and the environment around us will likely be tranquil and balanced. When life is unbalanced, however, we tend to become defensive because of unmet needs that create vacuums inside. Therefore, when others have better ideas, we feel threatened and become argumentative. We resort wholly to using the analytical left side of our brain because we do not have access to our imaginative and intuitive side—the right brain. Organizations need to have work/life promoting policies and support systems. And, leaders need to practice and support work/life balance in their own lives.

At Lilly, we survive and thrive in the business of discovering and developing innovative pharmaceutical products. To do this, we depend on our employees' brainpower and creativity, their initiative and their alignment with our goals for the business, and we need these at every level in the business. . . . A company can't hire just part of a person—you get the sore back along with skillful hands, you get the anxious heart along with educated and creative brain. So our policies and our programs will be effective only if we address this reality and if we acknowledge our employees for what they are—whole people. We should not just allow but encourage them to have lives beyond work.

—Randall Tobias, CEO, Eli Lilly and Company

Life outside work enriches our life at work. The more experiences we have in life, the more we have to draw from to make new connections and develop creative ideas.

THE FOURTH DIMENSION: COLLABORATIVE PEOPLE

Now we have an employee with an engaged mind, an updated knowledge base that has used its power of imagination to develop several creative ideas. The employee has a secure mind and has shared a new idea with managers and peers. The idea is a good one and appreciated by all. But like any raw idea, it needs to be developed. It will affect several areas in the organization. To develop the idea into a viable solution ready for implementation, it needs active collaboration between knowledgeable people from all affected areas (see Figure 4.6).

Collaborative Development

In today's fast-changing business environment, it is impossible for one person to keep up with all the changes and advancements.

FIGURE 4.6   Fourth Dimension of an Innovation and Performance Culture

People have to rely on others to catch what they may have missed. A collaborative environment ensures that the individual knowledge bases are pooled into a more comprehensive knowledge base. But there are at least two obstacles—personal and organizational—in achieving this goal. "Breaking down the silos" is a popular slogan repeated by business managers. But the biggest blocks to that effort are often the egos and organizational reward systems that reinforce the silos in managers' minds. Organizational incentives and reward systems tend to foster competition instead of collaboration.

> You have to listen carefully to all the smart people in the company. That's why a company like ours has to attract a lot of people who think in different ways, it has to allow a lot of dissent, and then it has to recognize the right ideas and put some real energy behind them.
>
> —Bill Gates, Chairman, Microsoft, *Fortune*,
> July 20, 1998

The day-to-day behaviors of company leaders set the tone for acceptance and collaboration. Mind generating ideas needs encouragement and support from the leader. Bob Palmer, Vice President of Operations for FedEx's Indianapolis regional hub has been known to ask employees, "What could we be doing differently to serve our customers better?" Executives at THQ, a video game company, have used similar leadership practices to tap into employees' creativity.

Two of the 10 Rules of Growth from THQ, the Video Game Company, recognized as one of America's fastest-growing companies (*Fast Company*, October 2000) are:

1. *Break the silence.* Create as many channels of communication as possible and use them as often as possible. Praise others often; don't boast of your own triumphs.
2. *Walk around.* The silence that creeps into large organizations can be broken by executives who wander throughout the company and who talk to workers directly.

If managers feel uneasy when others disagree with them, they create an environment in which others will only tell them what they want to hear, and there is no tapping of others' creativity. The key to unleashing creative ideas is to actively solicit ideas from employees at all levels in the organization.

Celebration and Fun

Leaders must create environments that not only challenge employees but encourage them to have fun and interact with others throughout the organization. Group fun and recreational activities involving various levels of management within and across departments are the best ways to tear down hierarchical barriers. It is easier to collaborate with people you know.

THE FIFTH DIMENSION: COMMITTED PEOPLE

For developed ideas to become innovations, they have to be applied throughout the organization. People who were involved in accepting and developing the idea will naturally be excited about implementing the change. But others who were not involved in the generation and acceptance steps, while intellectually understanding the need for change, may feel frightened by it on a personal level. Employees' commitment to the organization and commitment to their managers are the keys to overcoming this fear. A committed employee will say, "I don't fully understand this change. But, I trust my manager and am willing to give it a try. I know that if it doesn't work out, she will support me." One of the keys for FedEx's success has been the ability of its leaders to tap employees' discretionary effort, the difference between compliance and commitment. The leadership practices to create the previous four conditions—engaged people, growing people, secure people, and collaborative people—also lay the foundation for gaining employees' commitment. For example, explaining change in an effort to engage an employee also helps gain that employee's commitment. But the manager must do one more thing to gain commitment: build caring and mutually trusting relationships. At the FedEx Leadership Institute this is called the $R = D$ *principle* (Relationship = Discretionary Effort)—the difference between compliance and commitment (see Figure 4.7).

Throughout employees' careers, they will have many bosses. For some, they will do anything and for others just the minimum daily requirements. What is different about the boss for whom a person would do anything? A participant in one of my seminars answered that question this way: "I'll walk over hot coals for my current boss because he cares about me as a person."

Employees give their best to managers who are caring and sensitive to individual employee needs. If there is mutual trust between

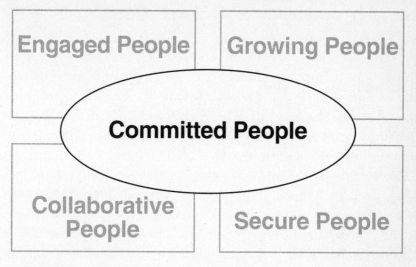

FIGURE 4.7 Fifth Dimension of an Innovation and Performance Culture

the employee and the manager, the employee will work hard to make the new idea a success and follow the leader into unknown territory even if the employee does not fully understand it.

During a leadership development class that I facilitated, I had the participants develop a personal coat-of-arms—a pictorial representation of their life values, goals, cherished experiences, and accomplishments. One of the questions the coat-of-arms addressed was "What has been your most fulfilling life moment?" Those who had a family invariably answered that it was the birth of their first child. A new manager shared with us a personal story from his previous employment. His wife was expecting their first child, and he got a call at work that she was in labor. He asked his boss for permission to go to the hospital and be with his wife. His boss asked him, "Are you a doctor? What are you going to do? Deliver a baby? You don't need to be there." Finally, very reluctantly, the manager (the antithesis of a caring boss) let him leave. Because of this incident, the new father decided to look for a new job and more understanding leader. Leadership, for both the leader and the follower, is often more an affair of the heart than of the head.

Putting It All Together

All five dimensions of the innovation culture support each other. An engaged mind is more receptive to learning and growing. Employees have an intrinsic need to learn and grow. And, when the organization and its managers actively support employees in meeting their growth needs, employees are motivated to become more engaged in the enterprise. Work/life balance leads to a balanced mind and a happy heart. Just as the mind is the instrument of knowledge, so is the heart the instrument of inspiration. Only the inspired heart of a manager can connect with and inspire the hearts of employees. Real leaders make emotional connections. A committed mind recognized for its role in the innovation process makes the employee feel good about herself and her manager. A committed mind goes above and beyond the call of duty in implementing new ideas for making a caring manager and the organization successful.

Leading for Innovation

Innovation is a people process. Managers at all levels of the organization must successfully fulfill the following five leadership responsibilities to create the conditions of a thriving innovation culture:

1. *Engage employees* in the enterprise and create clear expectations for active involvement in the innovation process.
2. Expect and help employees to *continually grow* their knowledge and skill bases.
3. Create a *secure environment* for expression and acceptance of creative ideas.

4. *Encourage collaborative* development of raw, creative ideas.

5. *Tap employees' commitment* for successful implementation of the developed ideas.

The next five chapters discuss the five leadership responsibilities in detail by introducing the leadership practices and behaviors that will show how leaders can:

- Make creative thinking and innovation a part of the design and infrastructure of the company instead of stumbling on ideas by chance.

- Learn how to create a clear, compelling, and understandable picture of why innovation is not an option but, in fact, an urgent and pressing need.

- Unleash the organization's competitive edge by developing and harnessing employees' creativity and commitment.

- Stay ahead of the competition by consistently designing and delivering superior customer value propositions (what the customer values when choosing among the available options).

- Engage employees in not only doing the job but also improving *how* the job is done.

- Create collaborative thinking across departments and disciplines.

- Focus every employee's sight on serving the customer.

Chapter 5

Engage Employees in the Enterprise

I've often thought—what is FedEx's secret weapon? I think I know. It's the EMPLOYEES. What a great group of dedicated and proud individuals. I observe your friendly faces and purposeful strides everywhere I go. FedEx is truly one of the best "people companies" in the world.
> —U.S. Senator David Pryor, in *How Time Flies*,
> a publication celebrating FedEx's 25th anniversary, 1998

Don Hardy, a colleague I have worked with closely for many years, had just returned from his assignment of heading FedEx Australia operations for two years. While there, he saw firsthand how FedEx's employees worldwide were fully engaged in the company's mission of doing absolutely, positively whatever it took to serve its customers. During Hardy's stay in Australia, one of his senior managers in Sydney, Kim Garner, met with a customer who sold duty-free goods to tourists. As part of this business, for an additional charge he would pack and ship the merchandise so his customers would not have to carry their purchases. His goal was to have the packages waiting for his customers when they returned home. FedEx was able to help him accomplish that feat Monday through Saturday, but he needed Sunday pickups—a service FedEx did not offer at the time—to achieve 100 percent customer satisfaction (see Figure 5.1).

In response to this customer request, Kim met with his staff to see if they could come up with a solution to this problem. The

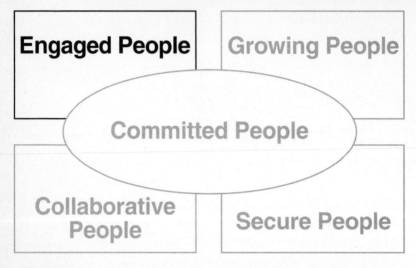

FIGURE 5.1   Innovation and Performance Culture: First Dimension

team brainstormed for a while until they worked out a viable plan to pick up this valuable customer's packages on Sundays. By going that extra mile, FedEx did not just keep this high-volume shipper; it actually saw an increase in business with the additional 50 to 200 packages the customer shipped every Sunday.

Don and Kim did not foist a plan on their employees. That would have meant using their employees' brawn but not their brains. Instead, they engaged their employees. This chapter discusses in detail how to fulfill the first leadership responsibility needed to create a thriving innovation culture.

ENGAGE EMPLOYEES AND CREATE A CLEAR EXPECTATION FOR THEIR ACTIVE INVOLVEMENT IN INNOVATION

As discussed in Chapter 4, engaging employees is all about communication. Leaders engage people by taking time on a regular basis to answer these questions:

- What is our business *growth* strategy?
- How is our business strategy *relevant* to what I do?
- What, *specifically*, should I do?
- How will it benefit me (meet my needs)?

The following leadership practices will help you and your employees find the answers to those questions. These practices are keys to fulfilling the first leadership responsibility: engaging employees.

- Share the company's strategies and goals in plain and simple language.
- Include employees at all levels in creating and keeping customers.
- Set measurable goals for improving your customer value propositions.
- Tell employees regularly how they are making a difference.

Share the Company's Strategies and Goals in Plain and Simple Language

A company's strategic plan and goals should not be limited to top executives and the board of directors. Every employee—from the CEO to the receptionist—should be privy to this information. But often, that is not the case.

When employees do not have a grasp of the company's direction, they have a difficult time deciphering what they should be working toward. Though it would appear to be a simple task, many companies fail to keep employees in the loop. This is a huge mistake.

FedEx has a well defined and elaborate process for communicating the company's business strategy. Information is provided through meetings, television broadcasts, the company's intranet, and printed pieces. Each officer of the company uses these mediums. In fact, the corporate communications department assigns communications specialists to each division to help managers make effective use of the tools available to them.

Officers and Directors Meetings

Even with myriad communication tools available, department managers have a primary responsibility to communicate the business strategy and plans in face-to-face meetings with employees. FedEx uses meetings with employees at all levels in formal and informal settings throughout the year to maintain ongoing conversations about its visions and goals.

The officers and directors meeting is a key annual meeting. At this meeting, the marketing department reports FedEx's performance against the competition. Here, the marketing senior vice president also shares marketing strategies for the coming year. This is followed by the chief financial officer's presentation on the company's performance, overall financial health, and fiscal year goals. In the afternoon, Fred Smith talks in detail about the larger business environment, his vision, and FedEx's business strategy for realizing this vision.

Blank cards are placed on everyone's table for writing any questions about the competitive environment and the company's growth strategy not answered in the various presentations. Fred and the senior management team take whatever time is needed to answer all questions. This in-depth group conversation with the senior management team gives everyone a thorough understanding of where FedEx is going and how it is going to get there. Perhaps more importantly, it instills confidence in the team at the top leading the charge.

While the annual meeting is important and informative, the all-day meetings at the division level during the days and weeks afterward are just as, if not more, important. In these meetings, the corporate strategic goals are translated into strategic initiatives. Again, an in-depth conversation is facilitated by division senior vice presidents to ensure that the division priorities and goals are fully aligned with the business strategy. Within a week of this meeting, all directors are expected to hold meetings with their staffs to make sure everyone, including the frontline employees, understands the business and division priorities for the coming year. In all the presentations, from that of the CEO to those of the department vice presidents, there is a common theme: Every department has to continually improve, in a measurable fashion, its contribution in each of the three People, Service, and Profit (PSP) areas.

Localizing the Message

Jim Petrie, Managing Director of Customer Service, was responsible for seven call centers located in Florida and Midwest, staffed with more than 1,100 customer service agents. The number of employees at each center ranged from 100 to 300. Jim made regular visits to all these centers. During interactions with small groups of customer service agents, he learned about business issues from their perspective and talked about the strategic initiatives of their department.

He encouraged the agents to ask pertinent questions: How is the company doing? How will these strategic initiatives help FedEx become more competitive? How will it benefit us? Jim also made it a point to share with them what was not working well. He set clear expectations for each work group and challenged them to work as a team to find new ways to better serve customers. It was these informal conversations with the customer service agents, not carefully prepared slides, that got the message across. Jim wanted to make sure the agents knew where we were going as a company and the critical role they play in helping FedEx get there. The actions required to achieve this goal were the basis for the MBO program (Management by Objectives) at the senior manager and the manager level.

Meetings also serve to get information to the frontline workers because most employees in the operations department do not work in offices or spend time at computers. The couriers spend most of their time on the road picking up or delivering packages. The package sorters in the hubs have to be at their assigned workstations during the sort. To keep these important employees up to speed on company developments, frontline managers hold brief meetings each day at the start of the shift to communicate important news of interest.

Using a Variety of Media

A key element of the comprehensive internal communication plan was FedEx's internal global television broadcast system. The system allowed employees to view:

- Short recaps every morning of the previous day's performance
- CEO and COO special broadcasts on strategic initiatives and acquisitions with call-in Q&A (e.g., to show how FedEx had become a family of companies serving customers' varied transportation and logistics needs)
- Executive management interviews and a call-in Q&A after quarterly and/or yearly earnings release
- Operational, leadership and other training

From the CEO and Chairman

Several times a year, everyone on the management team receives a newsletter titled "From the CEO." It begins with a review of the opportunities presented by the changing global business environment. It goes on to discuss FedEx's global growth strategy to take advantage of these trends. And, finally it lists the leadership responsibilities that every level of management has to fulfill to execute the growth strategy. In the June 2000 issue, Fred outlined his expectation that everyone be actively involved in the innovation process:

> Innovation has always been key to our success, but now it must be strategically focused toward customers, who are at the heart

of everything we do. To ensure that we're responsive to them and easy to do business with, we must be innovative and flexible. The new economy, revved by e-commerce, is fast, global and ultra-competitive. So we must innovate, particularly in e-commerce technology, by giving customers information about their goods in transit, enabling them to make up-to-second business decisions.

But innovation goes beyond the wired world. Real customer satisfaction is tied to innovation at all levels. For example, it applies to processes and solutions we develop in our jobs to serve customers.

Expect Everyone to Be Involved in Creating and Keeping Customers

Managers must start this practice by understanding the answers to three basic questions:

Q: In today's highly competitive business environment, how does any business increase its market share?

A: Business gains market share by creating and keeping more customers than the competitors.

Q: Who makes the final decision on which product or service to choose and how is that decision made?

A: The customer makes the final choice based on what he or she values—the customer value propositions.

Q: Who is responsible for creating and keeping customers?

A: Every employee in the organization is responsible for creating and keeping customers, either by designing value propositions to create customers or by delivering the value propositions to keep the customers.

This leadership responsibility expands the definition of innovation by making sure that every employee knows what the company's customer value propositions (CVP) are and that they understand business growth will require innovation across the board in every department, on every level.

Customer Value Propositions

Following are some common factors the customers value when making choices.

- Innovative products and services designed to meet each customer's unique needs.
- For business customers: Improving business models and enhancing their competitive edge resulting in revenue, productivity, or profit growth.
- For individuals: Improving life experiences, or saving time and offering peace of mind.
- Ease of use.
- Competitive price.
- Association with a respected, trusted brand.

We tend to forget who pays our salaries. It is the customer. We should remind ourselves constantly that we need to deliver what they want. And we need to be able to deliver different things to different customers. The minute we forget that, the reason for our being here is gone.

—Lars Nyberg, Chairman and CEO, NCR Corp.
Fast Company, October 2001

"A Satisfied Customer Made This Possible"

That phrase is printed on the front of FedEx paycheck envelopes to remind all employees that satisfying the customer is everyone's responsibility. The phrase makes the goal clear: 100 percent customer satisfaction after every interaction and transaction, and 100 percent service performance, ensuring that all deliveries are made within the time commitment for the service selected by the customer.

In the classes at the Leadership Institute, we discussed in detail why it was important to focus on 100 percent customer satisfaction rather than on some approximation of that percentage. Employees from at least five departments physically handle a domestic package between pickup and delivery. Even a 99 percent service level for each would result in only 95 percent of the customers receiving the package on time. With 3 million packages flowing through the system every night, 99 percent translates to 30,000 unhappy customers per day.

To keep FedEx's customer satisfaction level at 100 percent, the overall customer service measurement included 12 critical points in the value chain, or the elements of service that customers value. These elements helped the various departments and its employees see the part of the value chain their work directly affected. And, the measurement helped employees see how they were performing against the 100 percent customer satisfaction goal. This comprehensive measure of overall customer satisfaction and service quality was called Service Quality Indicator (SQI).

Table 5.1 lists the 12 SQI elements and the relative weighting factor assigned to each element. The weighting reflects the element's relative importance on customer satisfaction from the customers' standpoint. The SQI represents the delivery of FedEx's value propositions. Every company should have a comprehensive list of factors that define and measure customer satisfaction with its product or service.

At FedEx, the SQI was measured daily, and the results were reported organization-wide. In addition to the SQI, each operating division measured detailed process indices. Some of the measurements in the national hub operations included on-time arrivals and

TABLE 5.1　Deliver Customer Value Propositions

What the Customers Value: The Total Customer Experience (Customer Value Proposition)	Service Quality Indicator (SQI)	Weight
Phone call answered promptly by customer service. Packages picked up as requested and scheduled. Packages delivered on time.	Abandoned calls	1
	Missed pick-ups	10
	Right day late deliveries	1
	Wrong day late deliveries	5
	Overgoods (lost and found)	5
	Lost packages	10
Packages not damaged during shipment. Billed correctly the first time and proof of delivery provided on the invoice. Complaints resolved promptly and on first call.	Damaged packages	10
	Invoice adjustments Requested	1
	Missing proof of delivery	1
	Complaints reopened	5
	Traces (incomplete package scan data in the computer system)	1
International on-time delivery including customs clearance.	International SQI	1

departures of planes and trucks, unloading of airplanes within the defined standard, different sections of the sort operations completed on schedule, number of packages sorted improperly, sort rate per hour plan versus actual.

The package scans at every transfer point and other operational metrics gave FedEx a second-by-second snapshot of its performance that enabled improvement on a continuous basis. The continuous improvement teams used the data to achieve the 100 percent customer satisfaction goal.

An SQI can help individuals at various levels of an organization to see how their work affects the ability of the organization as a whole to deliver value to real customers. Compiling this data is hard work, but it opens up everyone's line of sight to real customers—the people who pay money for goods and services and are free to take their business elsewhere.

A survey conducted by Gallup found that 19 percent of the nation's workers not only aren't enthralled or excited by their work, they are "actively disengaged," meaning they are fundamentally disconnected from it . . . they don't know what is expected of them.

—The Gallup Organization, March 13, 2001

FedEx's emphasis throughout the organization is to provide an overall customer experience that appeals to both the head and the heart, Fred Smith told an audience at the J. D. Power and Associates Customer Service Conference in Santa Monica, CA, on November 13, 2003:

FedEx, for example, has always emphasized great customer service, but now that we offer a broad array of services beyond just express delivery, we are seeking to differentiate ourselves through an outstanding customer experience, which is broader than just service. Not surprisingly we're taking the holistic approach. We want to make sure that the customer has a great experience at every touchpoint—on the phone with our service reps, on the web site while trying to ship a package, at the front door when our courier delivers the package and at our service centers when dropping off a package. And not only do we look at the touchpoints, but we also pay attention to the life cycle of the customer's experience. We try to treat the customer royally, not only when we first get her business, but also when her business needs or package volumes change.

This leadership practice lays a solid case that everyone in the organization plays a role in designing and delivering company's customer value propositions and must be actively involved in the innovation process.

Set Measurable Goals for Improving Your Customer Value Propositions

In the business world, managers typically make pronouncements in speeches or memos proclaiming that employees need to think outside the box and innovate. These broad-stroke directives only leave employees wondering and waiting for direction because they have no specific goals or expectations. Using tools such as the SQI make it possible to align every person's responsibility and expectations for innovation with the elements of the organization's customer value propositions, offering a direct link from the employee to the customer.

The SQI element and the associated process measurements show every department where to concentrate its efforts. When employees know what customers expect and how far the company is from delivering it, creative tension develops for achieving that goal.

Department and Manager Objectives Aligned with Corporate PSP Objectives

FedEx has a very structured Management by Objectives program. Before the start of the fiscal year, corporate-level People, Service, Profit objectives are spelled out and communicated to everyone in the organization. From there, the senior vice presidents of each division spell out the division's PSP objectives in support of the corporate objectives, and on down the line to the department. Each objective at every level is aligned with the overall corporate PSP philosophy. The people objective is tied to the quality of leadership; the service objective is tied to improving service by reducing the SQI points. And the profit objective is tied to earnings and capital expenditures.

At the frontline manager and director levels, the objectives become specific and relate directly to the business processes under their control. Operating managers have engineering staffs assigned to be part of the continuous improvement teams; they actively participate in generating, accepting, and implementing ideas to meet the department's PSP objectives.

Shipments of Mother's Day Flowers

Each year, millions of mothers receive beautiful floral bouquets on Mother's Day. How do they get from the nursery to mom's front door? FedEx delivers them. In the early 1990s, the hub in Memphis was charged with reducing the number of damaged boxes in flower shipments originating from California. A team was assembled to look into this problem.

After following the flower boxes' process through the hub, it was determined that the boxes were getting jammed in the automated sort systems because they were too big. Normally, the boxes that could not be processed through the automated sort system were sorted manually. In addition to being costly, manual sorting was also very slow. During Mother's Day week the flower shipment volume was very heavy. And since Memphis was in the central time zone and two hours ahead of California, there was not much time between the arrival of a flight and the deadline for sorting the load before departure on the flights leaving for destination cities.

The manager invited a packaging engineer from the corporate packaging lab to be part of the problem-solving team. As a result, the group collectively came up with an innovative package design that could be processed through the automated sort system without damaging the box or its contents. The team worked with an account executive in California, who invited the major flower shippers to Memphis. After seeing the progression firsthand, they understood the effect manual processing would have on service. Since the new box was cheaper to produce than the original and could be processed automatically—therefore more quickly—shippers began to use it immediately. This is just one of the hundreds of creative ideas generated, accepted, and implemented every year across the organization because of specific objectives (MBOs) and the explicit expectations for everyone's involvement in the innovation process.

A payout at the end of the year for successfully achieving the objectives was icing on the cake. Each objective had a certain number of MBO points assigned to it and the dollar value for the point was declared at the end of the year. Part of the dollar value per point was determined by the successful attainment of corporate level PSP objectives.

Every employee also participated in profit sharing at Christmastime and at the end of the fiscal year. The amount of monies allocated to profit sharing was based on FedEx achieving the Profit goals set at the beginning of the year. MBOs, performance by objectives (PBOs) for professionals (similar to the MBO program for managers), and profit sharing played a key role in focusing employees' minds and engaging them in the enterprise.

Tell Employees Regularly How They Are Making a Difference

People need to know that they are making a difference. Managers must continually let employees know how they are helping the company create and keep customers and how that benefits the community at large. FedEx management recognizes that any one department cannot fulfill its responsibility without the close cooperation of other departments. Successful delivery of every package, every day of the year requires all departments in FedEx to work together to make sure the company keeps its promise. Because of this, managers regularly take time to meet with employees in other departments to let them know the difference they are making.

International Division Logistics Support

FedEx started primarily as a U.S.-oriented express company. But Fred knew that global trade was inevitable. After FedEx acquired Flying Tigers in 1989 to speed up its international expansion, every department worked feverishly to merge the Tigers' operations with FedEx's operations. This involved logistics support as well, including providing uniforms, airway bills, customer packaging supplies, spare parts, electronic gear, and other materials. My staff in materials and resource planning worked closely with the International division's planning staff based at the headquarters in Memphis. Skip Trevathan, Managing Director of Warehousing Operations and I arranged meetings with the operations management abroad at their facilities. This helped us understand their needs and how they were being met, and it gave us an opportunity to educate them on our capabilities. Most importantly, it established personal contacts, the key to generating, accepting, and implementing creative solutions with their needs in mind. The solutions developed were a combination of FedEx support systems and their support setup prior to the merger.

A few months after the merger, I got a call from Jim Wheeler, vice president of international planning requesting to attend my group's next all-employee meeting, which was held every three months. The meetings had three main objectives: (1) To have team members share ideas and be involved in the innovation process, which increased support for new products and services, (2) to update the group on the company's "state of the union," and (3) to have an officer provide feedback on our performance from the groups we supported. Jim shared with the group how the Tigers' integration was going and reported that the managers and operators in the field were pleased with the logistics support provided by our team. He relayed the importance of having the needed supplies to serve the customers and told them they were making an important contribution toward helping FedEx execute its international growth strategy. The group was presented with a plaque engraved with the message—Material and Resource Planning, for Outstanding Logistics Support to the International Division, July 1989.

One way the managers in any business can assess whether employees are actually engaged in the enterprise is to walk around and ask a random sample of employees the following questions:

- Where do we stand against the competition?

They should be able to answer, with both the customer value propositions, where the company is beating the competition and the areas that need improvement.

- What is the organization planning to do to address these areas of opportunity?

They should be able to cite specific initiatives at the corporate and their department level.

- What role are you playing in helping the organization enhance its competitive edge?

They should be able to convey a clear understanding of their role in executing the growth strategy and the relationship between their work and the company's customer value propositions.

While a car engine may be running, it will not move forward unless the engine is engaged. Similarly, for an organization to grow and move forward, employees must be engaged in the enterprise. Innovation—generation, acceptance, and implementation of creative ideas—comes from a group of people actively engaged in achieving shared goals.

Practical Ideas for Engaging Employees

- Devote at least one work group meeting each quarter to discussing the competitive environment, the company's strategy, and the previous quarter's performance.

- If some team members work in other locations, include them in work group meetings through video or telephone conference resources.

- Use all available communications media, such as newsletters, closed circuit television, and e-mail broadcasts, to keep reminding employees about the company's strategy and performance with particular emphasis on areas that must be improved.

- To maintain two-way communications, make sure employees' suggestions and recommendations for improvement are conveyed to those who should consider and possibly implement them.

- Make sure that sales and marketing circulate any non-confidential and nonproprietary information that will help employees understand what customers value, how they perceive their overall experience, and what needs to be done to improve it.

- Use the elements of your company's value propositions as common language across all departments and divisions.

TABLE 5.2 To Keep Innovating and Outperforming the Competition

Engage employees in the enterprise and create clear expectations for active involvement in the innovation process.				
1. Share the company's goals and strategies in simple and plain language.				
2. Include employees from all areas and at all levels in creating and keeping customers.				
3. Set measurable goals for improving customer value propositions.				
4. Tell employees regularly how they are making a difference.				

- Make sure that work group, departmental, and divisional goals are all aligned and directly related to improving customer service and the customer's experience.

- Recognize and publicize individual and group efforts toward improving the company's business processes and customer value propositions.

- Share a percentage of the company's profits with employees, making sure they understand how their efforts have contributed to the company's competitive edge (see Table 5.2).

Chapter 6

Expect and Help Employees to Continually Grow

Original ideas come from reassembling knowledge in new ways. But you need to have that knowledge in your mind before you can reassemble it.

—Leon Borstein, President, Bard College

Chapter 5 helped draw a line between an employee's responsibilities and their direct effect on the design and delivery of the company's customer value propositions. In this chapter, I define the knowledge and skills required for employees to develop innovative solutions (see Figure 6.1).

Innovation starts with the generation of ideas. The mind generates creative ideas by making connections between seemingly unrelated variables. The creative impulse springs from seeing new possibilities and new combinations. Although managers often say to employees, "We need to think outside the box," they do not really understand the conditions that must be in place for employees to do so.

To engage in creative thinking, the mind must have new dots—the result of an expanded knowledge base and a well developed natural capacity for imagination, or right brain thinking. For employees to think outside the proverbial box, two conditions

101

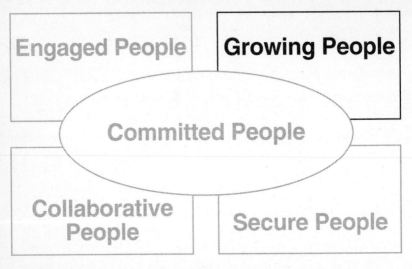

FIGURE 6.1   Innovation and Performance Culture: Second Dimension

must be present in the workplace. The first condition is having access to dots (knowledge base) outside the normal frame of reference. If the box is a department within the company, the dots outside the box represent knowledge of the total business processes within the company and outside the industry. If the box is technical knowledge, then the dots outside it are the latest technological advancements. The second condition is having employees with active imaginations (they use the right side of the brain to connect these dots). The leadership practices discussed in this chapter along with the outlined organizational support systems will help develop both of these conditions so that the mind can think outside the box.

The future belongs to those who have the ability to learn new skills.

—Bill Gates, CEO, Microsoft

EXPECT AND HELP EMPLOYEES TO CONTINUALLY GROW THEIR KNOWLEDGE AND SKILL BASES

The ability to create and connect new dots, and thus generate new and innovative ideas or solve problems creatively, must be embedded in an organization's day-to-day processes. But to create and connect these dots, employees must think differently about things using an expanded knowledge base. Organizational leaders can adopt the following practices to make this happen.

Leadership practices necessary to expand employees' knowledge bases:

- Require employees to update and expand their knowledge and skill bases.
- Provide resources and put support systems in place to facilitate growth and development.
- Actively participate in learning activities, especially right brain development activities.
- Hold employees accountable for updating their knowledge and skill bases.

REQUIRE EMPLOYEES TO UPDATE AND EXPAND THEIR KNOWLEDGE AND SKILL BASES

To contribute to the continual enhancement of the company's customer value propositions through innovative solutions, employees must have a deep understanding of varying customer needs and the changing business environment. Employees also need to be knowledgeable about the organization's total business processes, strategies, and the latest technological advancements in their fields.

Understanding Customer Needs and the Changing Business Environment

The rate of change in the business environment and customer needs is not going to slow down. Organizations must have defined processes and must devote resources to ensuring that the leaders at all levels of the organization understand customer needs and the changing business environment.

At FedEx, field visits help leaders keep apprised of changing customer needs and the correlating changes in the business environment. Once an employee reaches the rank of managing director, they are required to go on at least one field visit a year. The trips last two days. The first day, which is dedicated to working in the operations department, includes riding along with a courier making deliveries and pickups, and having conversations with the operations employees about the current business strategy. The second day is dedicated to making sales calls with local account executives. In-depth conversations with the customers, account executives, couriers, and the operations people provide an excellent education on the business environment and customer needs. The personal experience of being immersed in the daily workings at facilities, dealing firsthand with the systems, and hearing concerns expressed by the operators helped directors identify areas for improvement. They then share these ideas and concerns with the engineers responsible for designing the facilities and systems.

To emphasize the importance of staying in touch with the customers, every director is assigned a sales territory. The requirement is that they spend at least one day a quarter in the field making sales calls with the account executive in the assigned sales territory. A quarterly report is issued to the management team reflecting the activity in the previous quarter. Making more than the minimum number of sales calls is incentivised—employees who made the most sales calls are invited to join the top-performing account executives for the year-end president's club retreat at a resort.

The mechanics for this program are simple. Directors work with the account executives to select mutually convenient date(s). The account executive schedules the appointments and sends basic information about the customer. During my tenure, I made sales calls to a gold mining company in Montana, an international printing company in Virginia, and an engine manufacturer in Indiana. Whenever possible, the operations managers from the city station also joined in on the call.

During a sales call to the Circuit City distribution operations in Oklahoma, the team making the call learned that the director was very pleased with FedEx's service performance. At the time, Circuit City was using several transportation companies at the distribution center. When asked what FedEx could do to serve them better, he replied that changing the pickup time from early afternoon to late afternoon on Saturdays would yield more packages. The FedEx operations manager made the adjustment and later informed me that as a result, FedEx was picking up an additional 50 to 100 packages each day. While the additional business was great, the true benefit was a more complete and up-to-date picture of the business environment.

Today's customers are impatient and demanding. They have high expectations and very little time. So when you're trying to serve them, speed is critical. That means you need to shorten the distance between the people who create products and the people who buy products. That's a challenge when your manufacturers are in Japan, as ours are, and your customers are mostly in the United States. The Pacific Ocean is pretty wide—not only in terms of miles but also in terms of cultural distance. So, to get feedback about customer needs, we started the Lexus Owners' Advisory Forum in 1998. We bring about 20 engineers who are responsible for designing and producing the Lexus to the United States, and they meet with 15 or 20 loyal Lexus owners.

Together, they walk around the cars, and the customers tell the engineers what they like and what they dislike.

—Tony Fujita, Vice President of Parts, Service,
Customer Satisfaction, and Training-Lexus Division,
Toyota Motor Sales United States Inc.,
Fast Company, March 2000

Understanding the Organization's Total Business Processes, Strategies, and Plans

It is critical for all employees to understand not just the process for fulfilling their particular job responsibilities but the total business process from request for service or product to after-sale customer support. This knowledge will allow them to evaluate innovative ideas that could affect the total business process and customer experience. Because every organization has limited resources, it is vital that employees know and understand the current strategic priorities so that they can properly allocate resources thereby advancing the company's strategic priorities.

Typically, when managers and professionals think of training, they think of weeklong seminars at some far-off place. But in fact, most of the developmental activities needed to update the knowledge base do not require much out-of-pocket expense. The best learning experiences are on the job and not in the classrooms. Imagination is needed to develop and put in place plans that expose employees to processes across business units (e.g., rotating people through different divisions and across disciplines). Formal rotation programs that give employees real responsibilities help break down silos by building relationships and creating a "total business process" knowledge base.

Karl Birkholz, vice president, Memphis Hub Operations, told me that he rotated managers, senior managers, and the directors in the hub periodically. The extensive nightly operations in the hub required many processes to come together to launch the planes on time. Having hands-on experience in all areas of the hub broadened the directors' horizons, allowing them to gain deeper knowledge and appreciation of the entire operation. This in turn made it easier for them to share resources—the key to handling the changing package volume and product mix without hiring more people. In general, it made them more effective in evaluating and implementing new ideas for achieving the100 percent on-time departures and cost per package goals.

As Managing Director of Systems and Engineering, I supervised six managers who had more than 100 professionals in their groups. Most of the professionals had experience in multiple divisions of the company. FedEx had a strong promotion-from-within policy. All jobs were posted inside on the intranet, and any qualified employee from around the country could apply. This policy allowed the professionals to move from one division to another, and as a result they developed a comprehensive understanding of the overall business processes. Another equally important benefit was the networking and relationship-building opportunities the professionals had with peers in the other divisions. This created an environment for sharing, development, and implementation of innovative solutions for improving business processes. The managers had also come up through the ranks and had moved across disciplines and departments. In fact, a number of the directors, vice presidents, and senior vice presidents started their careers as couriers in the field or as sorters in the hub.

In today's information-driven economy, all employees, not just Information Technology (IT) specialists, must keep up with technological advancements that can improve process efficiencies and customer experience. FedEx uses several avenues to update the technical knowledge base of its employees.

One of those avenues entails encouraging active involvement in professional societies at the local and national level. Employees are urged to attend monthly dinner or lunch meetings of local professional organizations and their annual conferences. The presentations at these meetings offer excellent opportunities to learn about new achievements in transportation and other industries. Employees can expand their knowledge bases by studying industries outside their field.

> Leaders can also encourage people to broaden their horizons. Shortly after I came to Eli Lilly, I made a suggestion that our manufacturing people visit the Mars Candy Company and understand the manufacturing processes for making M&Ms. My thinking was that a single M&M has to be uniform in size and quality and is human consumable, which is also true of pills. But the pressures on cost control had always been greater in the candy business than in pharmaceuticals. So what could we learn? I think it caused people to think a little differently about our manufacturing processes, but even more important, it got them thinking about where else we could look to get ideas. We had historically benchmarked our operations against other pharmaceutical companies, which is fine. But it's often valuable to look for innovation at companies in other industries, to see what they have learned over time about processes that are similar to yours.
>
> —Randall Tobias, former CEO of Eli Lilly, interviewed by Peter Haapaniemi, a freelance writer for the *Unisys Exec* magazine, Volume 25, Number 2, 2003

Nearly every organization does something better than another in a given field. Organizations need to check out competition by using their services, to learn what the competition does better.

Professional certification in an employee's field is another avenue FedEx uses to keep knowledge bases up to date. In addition to encouraging employees to join professional societies, FedEx also encourages its employees to attain the certifications offered by these societies. Most professional societies have some form of certification process. Many managers at FedEx join their staffs in obtaining certification.

PROVIDE RESOURCES AND PUT IN PLACE SUPPORT SYSTEMS THAT FACILITATE GROWTH AND DEVELOPMENT

Professional Development Growth Plans

Another resource that motivates employees to continuously update their knowledge bases is having customized professional development and growth plans for each employee. FedEx uses the template shown in Table 6.1 to identify and chart the skills needed to

TABLE 6.1 Professional Development and Growth Plan

Employee_____   Date_____

Department/Function_____

Professional Development Growth Plan

Knowledge and skill bases needed to perform at the next level of responsibility and successfully execute FedEx growth strategy	Have demonstrated proficiency in the following areas	Gap between what is needed and have currently	Personal Development Plan to bridge the gap
Changing business environment and customer needs			
Technical skill and knowledge bases			
Managerial skills including business/strategic thinking			
Leadership and people skills			

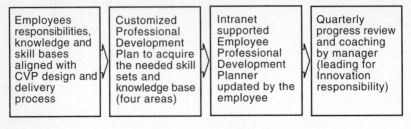

FIGURE 6.2   Support System for Facilitating the Learning Process

perform effectively and to also identify any gaps that may exist. The chart, which is kept on the company intranet and is updated by the employee, is used in a positive way as a tool to help the user prepare for the next level of responsibility. While employees may have graduated from top schools and possessed an adequate knowledge base when they were first hired, they need ongoing training and opportunities to stay on top of things. W. Edward Demming, the Total Quality Management guru, said, "No organization can survive with just good people. They need people that are improving" (*Khabar* magazine, March 2003). The focus of this development and coaching plan is not just to outline the skills needed now but to also identify the skills needed to execute the strategy that will carry the company forward.

At the beginning of each fiscal year, this plan is jointly developed by the employee and his or her manager. Once a quarter, the employee updates the plan and schedules a meeting with the manager to review progress. Depending on the skills that need improvement, a manager may coach the employee or use other resources within and outside the company (see Figure 6.2).

This system automates the company's process for facilitating growth and development for each employee, and puts employees in charge of their own professional growth and development. Being able to access online the plans of all employees also allows the Human Resources department to assess the training needs at the organizational level. Instead of offering the same courses year after year, Human Resources can modify existing courses and develop new courses to meet current strategic business needs.

> Trouble is, technical knowledge today has the shelf life of fruit. It's very easy for companies and even entire countries to fall behind in understanding, applying, and creating new technology.... Consider a continuously successful company that holds a commanding share of its market by virtue of delivering differentiated, customer-responsive products, created by highly skilled engineers, who are directed by a forward-looking management team and funded by a substantial investment in R&D.... A half century ago, Winston Churchill observed, "The empires of the future are the empires of the mind." He was pointing out that tomorrow's growth will come not from hoarding raw materials but from harnessing intellectual capital. Ideas and inventions, knowledge and know-how allow us to build better tools, life enhancing technologies, more productive processes, and self-managing, self-repairing infrastructures that automate much of the drudgery of life.
>
> —Mike Ruettgers, Executive Chairman,
> EMC Corp., CBS. MarketWatch.com
> "Outside the Box" commentary, November 21, 2001

Coaching Employees to "Sell" Their Creative Ideas

In addition to updating their knowledge bases, professionals, especially technical professionals, must know how to sell new ideas. Every creative idea involves some deviation from the status quo and accepted way of doing things. That usually means that the people who are to embrace it will feel some discomfort. What is more, it is bound to draw resistance from employees who must implement it, especially if they were not involved in generating the idea. To minimize this resistance and increase the chances for acceptance of creative ideas, professionals need to learn how to present (sell) their ideas to others. Technical professionals often believe that if the benefits of implementing the new ideas are logical and spelled out on paper, then others will automatically jump on board and support the idea. Through several firsthand experiences, I learned the hard way that the numbers alone will not sell creative cost-saving ideas. Feelings play an equally important role.

While working at RCA Records as Manager of Distribution Systems in Indianapolis, I developed a cost savings proposal to automate the manual pick and pack operations in the distribution center. I gave a copy of the proposal to my boss, Dale Whitehurst, Vice President of the business unit, and to the Director of Operations, Paul Finn for their review and input. My boss loved the idea and immediately set up a meeting with his boss Dave Heneberry, who was Executive Vice President of RCA Music Service in the New York corporate offices. Dale, Paul, and I flew to New York to present the idea to Dave. After listening to my presentation, Paul said that overall he liked it, but that there were some issues he was not clear on—definitely not a sign of a united front from our team. Dave told us that we had some more work to do before he could give his approval. Obviously, I had not sold Paul on the idea before we made the presentation.

My boss asked me in detail how and when I got Paul involved in the idea development process. He coached me on the people (feeling) side of selling ideas. He suggested that before circulating ideas to the world on paper as fully developed, official proposals, I should have an informal conversation with those directly affected, where I could run the ideas past them and ask for their thoughts. That way, I would get the benefit of the knowledge base of others and would make them feel part of the innovation process right from the start. I used this approach to involve Paul early in the ideas generation process, and we both began presenting ideas to Dale and Dave as joint ideas, a collaborative effort between planning and operations. I passed this early lesson on to the engineering managers in my group at FedEx.

Knowledge Sharing and Coaching by Executive Management

In 1989, the operational integration of Flying Tigers into FedEx was in full swing. Both Flying Tigers and FedEx transported dangerous goods (DG) on their airplanes. FedEx containerized the dangerous goods shipments while Flying Tigers palletized their DG shipments. A study was underway to decide which mode of DG transportation to implement system wide. Floyd Fisk, an engineer from my group, was one of the three engineers assigned to work on this study.

I had just moved into my new position as managing director of System Form Engineering. The engineers had issued an interim report on their research a week before. Fred Smith's office scheduled a meeting to go over the report. So, on my second day in the new position, I found myself sitting in the conference room next to Fred Smith's office. At the beginning of the meeting, I introduced myself as the new director of the group and told Fred I was there to learn. He had read the entire 20-page interim report. He was asking questions, and the engineers were presenting their rationale about the data and analysis in the report. After saying he wanted to make sure the group considered all the factors impacted by this important decision, he got up and started drawing on the board. He walked us through the floor plans and load configurations for each aircraft type in FedEx's fleet. Dangerous goods could only be loaded in the designated load positions. Fred Smith is a pilot. He discussed in detail the responsibilities of pilots carrying dangerous goods. He talked about the different container and pallet types, their capacities, and other technical and operational factors.

I knew that Fred was a strategic and visionary leader. But I had no idea about his grasp of the technical and operational details. It was incredible that he took 30 minutes from his busy schedule to educate us. This knowledge sharing and coaching by Fred gave us a thorough understanding of all the factors we needed to take into account. As a result of this crash course, I was able to help the team in its analysis and final recommendation to carry DG in containers.

Allocating the Needed Resources for Ongoing Training

During tight economic times, often the first things to be slashed from budgets are travel, new hires, and training. During good economic times, senior management frequently does not provide the needed resources for training either—time and money. Usually, the simple reason for the lack of resources is that middle managers have done a poor job educating their superiors about this critical business need. Ongoing training can only be accomplished by developing and presenting a comprehensive talent development strategy that directly relates professional development needs and plans to successful execution of the company's business growth strategy.

What businesses must understand is that providing innovative solutions to meet customer needs and reducing the cost of doing business are paramount during both boom and bust times. "Our people are our most important asset" is not just a catchy slogan, it is the truth. Managers must understand, at the deepest level, that the knowledge, experience, and commitment of employees drive a company. And, it is the application of that knowledge and experience in developing innovative solutions that gives an organization a competitive edge. Therefore, it is imperative for managers to be aware that updating employees' knowledge and skill base is an investment; it enhances the value and output of a company's most valuable asset (employees) and should not be looked on as an expense.

Employees have a need to grow. And if the organizations where they are employed do not provide that opportunity, the employees will leave when another company presents such a growth opportunity. When knowledge workers leave, it not only results in turnover costs but also reduces the company's capacity for innovation.

> Look, tech is a people-intensive industry, not a capital-intensive industry. You lose your engineers, you lose your software designers, your chip designers, and your key sales executives, and you are going to be in a world of hurt when things turn around.
>
> —Ed Zander, Managing Director Silver Lake
> Partners and former President and COO of Sun
> Microsystems in Business 2.0, July 2003

PARTICIPATE IN LEARNING ACTIVITIES (ESPECIALLY WHOLE BRAIN THINKING DEVELOPMENT ACTIVITIES)

Much of the time in the business world is spent in analyzing numbers—productivity, budgets, and sales quotas. As a result, the analytical, left brain is reasonably well developed, and high-powered executives often have mastered those skills. In most cases, what is missing at that level are strategic thinking skills and right brain (imagination) thinking. If the CEO takes the lead and gets personally involved in expanding his mind, it sends a powerful message to the entire organization. Talking about what he is learning sets an example for his direct reports to follow and so on down the organization.

Exploring What-Ifs

In all-day meetings with Tom Oliver, Executive Vice President at FedEx, we reviewed step by step the overall customer experience with the company. He would pose hypothetical situations that included scenarios where information on the airway bill would be missing. We would have to evaluate the effect that scenario would have on customs clearance and our service commitment. We talked through how we would handle those situations to ensure that we were creating the most satisfying customer experience.

This what-if thinking covered not only the delivery of the shipment on time but the pre- and postdelivery process (billing, customer queries, proactive notification), guaranteeing that FedEx had a system in place to handle such situations, thereby making the customer experience a positive one. The Operations Research group and my group, System Form Engineering, spent more than half our time developing and evaluating what-ifs posed by Fred Smith.

Hosting Guest Speakers from Different Fields

Most departments at FedEx have onsite or off-site planning sessions. At the Leadership Institute's quarterly planning sessions, FedEx always had a speaker from outside the company, usually a professor or a training consultant expert in experiential learning who would engage the entire group in experiential learning exercises.

People need experiences at "getting out of the box" if they are to do so when it matters. One interesting approach is practiced by CEO Lou Gerstner at IBM. Every six weeks he takes his top 40 managers off-site for a two-day retreat. But these are not typical operating reviews. Rather, they are dedicated to management learning in nontraditional areas. Each session features an outside speaker who addresses a topic that is peripheral to the immediate concerns of IBM's leadership. These speakers may be academics, executives from other industries, or even representatives of the art world. Gerstner personally leads these sessions; his objective is to give his executives practice in stretching their thinking and developing new perspectives on IBM's business.

—Michael Hammer and Steven A. Stanton, "The Power of Reflection," *Fortune*, November 24, 1997

If senior managers place themselves in learning situations, it sends a powerful message to everyone in the organization. And it greatly increases the probability that the employees will follow. Not only that, but senior management can help by being actively involved in sharing their knowledge and experience with new managers.

HOLD EMPLOYEES ACCOUNTABLE FOR UPDATING THEIR KNOWLEDGE AND SKILL BASES

In addition to annual performance reviews, FedEx has several other measurement systems that track performance and learning in each of the three critical areas of the PSP culture.

Survey Feedback Action (SFA)

Each year at FedEx, employees anonymously fill out a special survey. It measures the managers' and organization's effectiveness in all critical areas with special emphasis on day-to-day leadership behaviors. The survey measures, among other things, the company's effectiveness in keeping employees engaged in the enterprise and helping them grow with observations that include:

- My manager helps us do our jobs better.
- I have enough training to do my job well.
- My manager and manager's boss keep us informed.

Aside from these kinds of ratings, the survey also provides an area for feedback, which is the most useful tool for managers to draw from. After receiving the survey results, every manager meets with his team to determine why they responded as they did, and to come up with an action plan to address their concerns. This plan is then followed and progress reviewed monthly in the staff meetings.

Individual Performance Review

Performance reviews for both the managers and individual contributors include a space for feedback on specific categories for personal development and growth in the knowledge and skills areas previously discussed. Also included is a growth planner for acquiring knowledge, skills, and abilities to perform at the next level. This planner also lists specific areas for knowledge expansion with associated activities and implementation dates. At the performance review, the manager reviews not just the performance but also the progress on the growth planner.

To reinforce the expectation that every employee is responsible for updating his or her knowledge and skill base, any employee performance reviews should include the following two questions:

1. *How are you more valuable to the company than you were a year ago?* Employees should be able to answer with specific examples of growth in two or more of the four key knowledge areas — business processes, technological advancements, industry knowledge, and changing customer needs. They should be able to cite the collaborative relationships they have developed with other departments and functions in the organization. Employees should be able to cite new managerial or leadership skills they have acquired that play a vital role in the generation, acceptance, and implementation of creative ideas.

2. *How is the company better, more competitive, this year than last year because of your contributions?* Employees should be

able to describe how they contributed innovatively in one or more of the three steps in innovation—generation, acceptance/enhancement, and implementation. If the employee is a manager, she should be able to cite measurable improvement in one or more of the elements of the organization's customer value proposition as a result of her group's work over the past year.

For managers of managers, the following question should be included:

3. *Using the innovation leadership responsibilities and practices as criteria, in what ways are the managers under your direct supervision better leaders this year compared with a year ago because of leadership development coaching that you have provided?*

Managers should be able to cite specific ways they coached those reporting to them to overcome whatever deficiencies may have been identified in the company's annual leadership effectiveness surveys.

Benefits Quality Forum

The FedEx's Benefits department organized a Quality Forum for the over 200 employees in the department and the vendors who provided benefits-related services to FedEx. The objectives for this forum were:

- Learn about the benefits industry from the experts in the industry. This was accomplished by having CEOs and other senior officers from leading benefit companies such as Vanguard, Cigna, and others speak to the group.
- Have frontline employees build good working relationships with vendors in order to develop innovative solutions. This was achieved by reserving one day for team-building activities.

- Learn about what other large companies are doing. This was achieved by having representatives from large companies and research department employees of service providers make presentations and participate in panel discussions.

- Promote innovation by publicly recognizing the companies who worked with FedEx in generating, accepting, and implementing cost savings and service-enhancing ideas.

Like the costs at any large company, employees' benefits expenditures at FedEx account for a large and growing part of the operating expenses running into the billions of dollars. Even a small reduction in these expenses translates into millions. Many creative ideas, big and small, were generated, developed, and implemented as a result of the updated knowledge base and improved collaboration between the vendors and FedEx benefits department employees.

FedEx was instrumental in forming the Memphis Business Group on Health that would increase buying power so that FedEx could negotiate lower premiums on employees' health coverage. Fred liked the idea and met with his counterparts, the other CEOs in Memphis, to discuss the idea. Shortly after that meeting, the group was formed and negotiated lower prices for employees' health coverage.

Ongoing Professional Development

Employees feel better about themselves and are capable of adding more value when they grow and develop personally and professionally. Employees have a need to grow. If they do not have growth opportunities where they work, they will seek employment where they think they can grow.

When knowledgeable workers leave, an expanded knowledge base of information about the industry leaves with them. The total business process knowledge leaves with them. The relationships developed and nurtured over the years leave with them.

When times are tough and a company is falling short of its profit targets, it may be necessary to slash travel, hiring, and training budgets temporarily. But if the training freeze goes on for an extended time, the individual and collective knowledge base will have stopped expanding. It reduces the company's future innovation capacity. It is difficult, when focused on the next quarter earning numbers, to see the long-term adverse impact of this freeze, but a thriving innovation culture requires continually updated knowledge and skill bases.

Ally & Gargano, an advertising agency, was responsible for the innovative and memorable ads that helped FedEx become a household name. Its founder Carl Ally summarized beautifully the importance of an updated and expanded knowledge base in generating creative ideas. He said, "The creative person wants to be a know-it-all. He wants to know about all kinds of things: ancient history, nineteenth-century mathematics, current manufacturing techniques, flower arranging, and hog futures. Because he never knows when these ideas might come together to form a new idea. It may happen six minutes later or six months down the road. But he has faith that it will happen" (Quoted in *Wisdom, Inc.* by Seth Godin, p. 22, Harper Business, New York, 1995).

The following example shows how FedEx's Finance division helped professionals and managers grow their knowledge and skill bases by using the four leadership practices discussed in this chapter.

Learning Institute in the Finance Division

Ed Chady joined FedEx in 1982 as a financial analyst and retired in 2003. His last position at FedEx was managing director of Special Projects and Training in Revenue Operations. Shortly after joining FedEx, Ed got involved in designing a professional and personal development process. It started with Ed and several other individual contributors, thinking out loud,

"What do we need to learn to develop and realize our full potential?" They agreed on a goal-oriented development process built around answering the following three questions:

1. What do I need to learn to add maximum value in my current position?
2. What do I need to learn to be successful at the next level?
3. What do I need to learn to improve myself as a person?

"We named it an Individual Development Planner (IDP) instead of a training plan because we wanted the focus on learning as a personal responsibility as opposed to somebody teaching you." These early discussions eventually led to the establishment of a Finance Learning and Development Center (FLDC) in the late 1990s.

Early development of the IDP concept took place in the early 1980s when technological advancements in software and hardware were being introduced at a fast pace. Therefore, the answer to the first question for most people was learning to use the latest software and learning more about the operational area of the company they were supporting. For most people, the answer to the second question was about learning managerial and leadership skills. The answer to the third question varied widely (e.g., be a better speaker; give back to the community by volunteering at the Special Olympics).

The manager was intimately involved in helping employees explore answers to the three questions and talked them through to make sure the plans were realistic and had a time frame for executing each element. He provided the needed support in terms of time and budget. Employees bought into the concept because they were driving the process.

An important by-product of this process was stronger commitment from the employees to the organization and their managers. It opened their eyes to other parts of the company and helped nurture new ways of thinking. Ed explained, "We integrated the IDP into the overall corporate culture. One of the 10 items on the corporate performance review was 'Self-Development and Appraisal—Improves own capabilities to meet changing demands and job requirements.' We used the employee's performance on the personal and professional development planner as the resource for rating this self-development item.

"We also provided a carrot by making learning one of the MBOs or PBOs. Successful completion resulted in a pay out semi-annually, if the corporation as a whole met its overall People-Service-Profit objectives. By making this a component of the MBO process, it allowed us to put stretch in this objective by suggesting areas of knowledge and skills for including in their planners.

"Another learning activity we engaged in as a group was brown bag lunch once a week. I'd buy a copy of a recently published book on business thinking, leadership, and other subjects for each team member. We would all read a chapter before the meeting and share our thoughts during the brown bag lunch. This allowed the people in my group to see that I'm here to listen. And, this in turn made them feel comfortable in sharing their creative ideas about the work, that is, ideas for improving our internal processes and serving our customers better. These informal lunch discussions made the group a stronger team."

In the mid-1990s, new skills development and enhancement were needed in a much broader way. This led to the institution of the FLDC. The Institute's main objective was to source training courses, videotapes, audiotapes, books, and speakers, or develop these to respond to the growing demands for skills development

TABLE 6.2   To Keep Innovating and Outperforming the Competition

Engage employees in the enterprise and create clear expectations for active involvement in the innovation process.	Expect and help employees continually grow their knowledge and skill bases.			
1. Share the company's goals and strategies in simple and plain language.	1. Require employees to update and expand their knowledge and skill bases.			
2. Include employees from all areas and at all levels in creating and keeping customers.	2. Provide resources and put support systems in place.			
3. Set measurable goals for improving customer value propositions.	3. Actively participate in learning activities.			
4. Tell employees regularly how they are making a difference.	4. Hold employees accountable for updating their knowledge and skill bases.			

within the Finance division. Other departments also saw the need for or had independently developed a similar concept, and resource sharing and benchmarking were used both within and outside the corporation to maximize resources.

The Finance Learning Institute and Ed Chady helped professionals and managers in Finance grow their knowledge and skill bases by using the four leadership practices summarized in Table 6.2.

PRACTICAL IDEAS FOR KEEPING EMPLOYEES' KNOWLEDGE AND SKILL BASE CURRENT

- Stay close to your customers. Involve them in every stage of the product or service design process. Build it with them and they will come.

- To understand changing customer needs, schedule managers and employees to make sales calls or work on the retail floor once every six months.

- When it is difficult or impractical to schedule sales calls, invite sales associates to brief you and your staff on what customers have been saying recently about your products or services, especially compared with those offered by competitors.

- To help your employees understand and improve your company's business processes, schedule employees to spend time observing or working in each department.

- Invite vendors and suppliers to make presentations on new products and services as well as on advancements and trends in their respective fields.

- Cross-train your employees whenever possible. Have each one share knowledge and skills with at least one other person.

- Expect employees who attend conferences, conventions, seminars, or workshops to share what they learned with others through formal presentations and lunchtime discussions.

- Hold employees accountable for professional growth and development by requiring them to develop and adhere to a professional development plan.

- Model the way by being curious, inquisitive, and an avid reader of a wide range of books and periodicals. Share important passages and articles with your colleagues.

- Ask employees to leave recent magazines and journals, with articles of particular relevance flagged, in common areas.

Chapter 7

Create a Secure Environment for Expression and Acceptance of Creative Ideas

A stressed mind is in a survival mode. A stressed mind is not in a creative mode.

—Don Hardy, Former Managing Director,
FedEx Operations in Australia

The competitive edge lies with companies whose management provides the leadership essential to building and sustaining an innovation and performance culture. Managers' day-to-day behaviors play a key role in motivating employees to give the gift of their discretionary effort—enthusiasm, creativity, and commitment—to the organization. Up to this point, this book has addressed how to engage people in the enterprise, help employees grow their knowledge base, and generate creative ideas. This chapter addresses how to share these ideas (see Figure 7.1).

What does it take to express new ideas?

- Belief that the organization wants new ideas from everyone.
- Formal and informal ways to express new ideas.

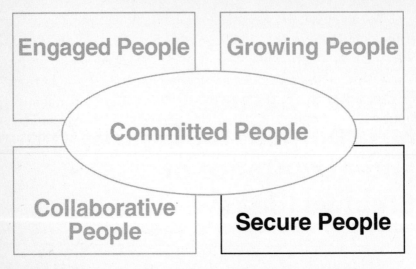

FIGURE 7.1   Innovation and Performance Culture: Third Dimension

- Belief that someone will take the expressed ideas seriously.
- Belief that one will get credit for new ideas and maybe a reward.

It is vital that employees feel secure in expressing their ideas. Managers, in turn, must feel secure in accepting new and unfamiliar ideas, especially if the ideas expressed are different than theirs. Feelings of security must be present in both the external and the internal environments. Externally, a secure workplace environment promotes the feeling that ideas are welcome, even if they are contrary to current assumptions. The environment must convey to employees that they are permitted, in fact, encouraged to voice ideas even if they are in conflict with the bosses' views. Both for managers and employees, inner security is a by-product of a fulfilling life on and off the job. On the job, it means having updated knowledge and skill bases to successfully meet challenges and responsibilities that lead to professional competence and accomplishment.

Most companies have a mission statement to remind everyone in the organization why it exists—its purpose—usually a description of the product and services provided to customers. The mission statement also provides a foundation for strategic thinking and for developing the organization's growth strategy and initiatives. Along with a mission statement, companies should develop and disseminate a permission statement that promotes thinking, sharing, acceptance, and implementation of innovative ideas.

Most employees need to hear, and to believe, that the boss won't bench them if they swing at a ball on a 3–1 pitch . . . you don't want a permission statement just to avoid getting hung up on little things. You want one to create the opportunity to do big things. Permission statement: a set of principles—some articulated, some tacit—that allows people to act on their own for the good of the company. What should a permission statement offer? Here's my list:

- Permission to think (and voice) conflicting ideas.
- Permission to reflect—that is, to take a step back from the urgent and spend a day on the important.
- Permission to collaborate—within a department or outside it, without clearing it in advance.
- Permission to disagree.
- Permission to be different.
- Permission to invent (experiment).

> —Thomas Stewart, "Just Think: No Permission
> Needed," *Fortune*, January 8, 2001

The permission culture plays a key role in meeting the human need for developing and expressing creative ideas, the self-actualization need, the highest level in Maslow's need hierarchy.

After studying creative and accomplished people such as Albert Einstein, Jane Addams, Eleanor Roosevelt, Frederick Douglas, and others, Abraham Maslow developed a hierarchy of needs. He described five primary sets of needs that motivate human behavior: physiological, safety/security, love and belongingness, esteem, and self-actualization. These needs are arranged in a hierarchical fashion because the basic survival needs must be satisfied before others can be addressed.

The basic physiological needs are food, water, air, and shelter. The needs for physical safety and psychological security are next on the ladder. The human need to love and be loved by others and to belong to groups forms the basis for the love and belonging needs. Esteem needs consist of the desires for reputation and respect from others. Self-actualization includes the experience of feeling that a person is developing his or her potential in a multidimensional way: personal, social, occupational, and spiritual. At work it means making creative contributions.

A manager must encourage and reward creative ideas and risk taking to create a secure and safe environment for employees to express ideas. Employees must understand that whenever a new idea is tested there is a risk that it may not work as planned. Managers must let employees know that they fully embrace the potential for failure as a natural part of the innovation process.

FedEx measures the feeling of security about the job in its annual employees survey (SFA; see Chapter 6), with the measure "I can be sure of a job if I do good work."

Off the job, personal satisfaction comes principally from spiritual pursuits, recreational activities, and our relationships with family and friends.

Over the past decade, much has been said about life balance, and it has been defined in many ways. The concept I have tried to use in my life is simply finding the time and energy to engage in all the activities that make life joyous, meaningful, and fun—in other words allocating personal time and energy to celebrate life in its fullness.

As we assume more responsibilities at work and in our personal lives, our needs and goals compete for the limited personal resources of time and energy. They also conflict with each other as well as with the reality of the outside world. Psychological studies have shown that inner conflicts are the primary source of dilemmas. Unresolved inner conflicts do not go away, they create stress.

STRESS INTERFERES WITH THE INNOVATION PROCESS

Stress can come from any area of life—on the job and off the job. Like the tension in a guitar string, just the right tension produces beautiful music, but too much snaps the string. In a similar vein, challenges and deadlines at work keep us sharp and on our toes. However, when there is too much to do and not enough time to do it, corners are cut and burnout occurs.

Demands at work that exceed our ability to meet them can create stress. An overly stressed mind is not conducive to creative thinking, or generating the what-ifs required for innovation. A stressed mind has a low tolerance for frustration and is not receptive to new ideas especially when they are at odds with the status quo. The first step in creative problem solving in business is to understand the total picture—all the contributing factors and the effect a particular problem has on the business process. A stressed and agitated mind produces a distorted picture.

A *Time* magazine story titled "Stress and the Superdad," August 23, 2004, reported, "Of the 1,302 men polled, 75 percent said they were concerned about keeping up with changing job skills, and even among those 25 to 34, a presumably more tech-savvy cohort, 79 percent admitted to such concerns." By successfully fulfilling the leadership responsibility of helping employees continually grow their knowledge and skill base, discussed in Chapter 6, managers can help minimize this concern on part of the employees.

It is abundantly clear that what happens to people off the job affects performance on the job as well. Neither the organization nor people can continue to look at work and career in isolation from employees' lives outside work. Because the growth and productivity of organizations are more dependent than ever on the effectiveness of human performance, corporations that choose to ignore this do so at a great cost to themselves. It is in the organization's self-interest to help managers and employees lead a balanced life. Not having enough time to nurture and enjoy the relationships we value in life can create stress that carries over to workplace performance. Because of this, the new breed of managers and employees are different from their predecessors. The economic manager is being superseded by the psychological manager, for whom Maslow called "the higher needs" have become important.

When people's material needs are satisfied, their needs for challenging and significant work, for fulfilling relationships, and for stimulating and fulfilling life experiences become prime motivating factors. When these needs are not met, frustration and stress set in.

Organizations that cannot respond to people as total human beings will stagnate and become less creative than those organizations better able to assist people successfully achieve their career and personal work/life balance goals.

In the twenty-first century, the return on investment (ROI)—the bottom line measurement—is directly related to:

- Return on Ideas and Innovation: Employees' ideas for improving the company's customer value propositions and customer experience are the keys to creating customers and improving market share. Employees' ideas for improving business processes help reduce the cost of doing business.

- Return on Initiative: Employees' initiative in implementing the creative ideas and delivering company's value propositions helps keep customers.

- Return on Interpersonal Relationships: Collaborative relationships within the company and outside the company are the keys to developing and implementing innovative solutions to stay ahead of the changing business environment. Collaborative relationships with customers help keep the lines of communication open and minimize the risk of losing customers to the competition. Collaborative relationships with suppliers ensure quality material at most economical prices.

The realities of today's workplace are:

- Two thirds of mothers with children at home are working outside the home.

- Dual-career couples report feelings of chronic fatigue and lack of time.

- Asked to select the most important goal for the women's movement today, participants in a Time/CNN poll rate "helping women balance work and family" as number one.

- Employees in the so-called sandwich generation, who care for both children and aging parents, have extra demands on their time.

Dr. Stephen Rechstschaffen, author of *Time Shifting: Creating More Time to Enjoy Your Life* (New York: Doubleday, 1996), claims that 95 percent of the stress in our lives relates to our feeling of time poverty; it is the feeling that we cannot possibly accomplish all that we have to do because there is not enough time. Whether it's 95 percent or something less, lack of time is a major stress factor in today's fast-paced and demanding lifestyle.

All this highlights the need for managers to be sensitive to the realities of their employees' lives. But managers can only be fully sensitive to their employees' work/life balance concerns if they are paying attention to their own work/life balance.

INTERFERENCE FROM EGO

One of the biggest and most often unacknowledged obstacles to accepting new and different ideas is the human ego. It is a fact of life that all people have one, and as they go up the corporate ladder, their ego often becomes bigger. Intellectually, people understand that others think differently, and that diverse thinking generates new perspectives, new insights, and new approaches to solving business problems. But emotionally, humans—driven by an active ego—are uncomfortable when someone else thinks in a different way. And the moment a person finds what appears to be the right answer, the mind gets the signal to stop looking for new information and stop listening to other ideas. This stifles creativity in the organization.

> Ego is the number-one killer of good decision-making processes within companies. Teams work better when individual members check their egos at the door. I'm not proposing that we should be automatons, but if we all had a little less ego, the overall system would work much better than it does.
>
> —Bo Peabody, Cofounder and Chairman, Village Ventures, Williamstown, MA, *Fast Company*, April 2002

How does one keep the ego in check? A balanced life, allowing time for psychological and spiritual growth is key when addressing this issue. A balanced life requires supportive relationships and a spiritual foundation to provide an expanded base for self-worth where career is still an important part of life's balance.

Most treat work/life balance as an option—a nice idea, but not a necessity. But people pay a huge price in all areas of their lives, especially those that matter most—leadership effectiveness, health, and relationships—when they choose to ignore it.

CREATE A SECURE ENVIRONMENT FOR THE EXPRESSION AND ACCEPTANCE OF CREATIVE IDEAS

The following leadership practices and support systems are needed for fulfilling this responsibility:

- Develop and sustain a permission culture.
- Let employees know that you fully embrace the potential for failure as part of innovation.
- Integrate "Leading for Innovation and Balance" in leadership development.
- Practice and support balance.

Develop and Sustain a Permission Culture

Steve Stapleton was the first Director of Sales Planning and Administration at Federal Express in the early 1980s when FedEx was experiencing double-digit growth. Package volumes were growing rapidly. At the same time, customers were complaining that they did not have time to complete the necessary paperwork for shipping with FedEx. Steve supported Corporate Sales' efforts to respond to the field Sales organization and field operations that FedEx must develop an automation device to assist customers with air waybill and document preparation, especially for large volume and multipiece shippers. Craig Bell, Vice President of Sales, approached senior management for permission to have Steve and Corporate Sales assume the lead in pursuing this critical need. Over the next weeks and months, Steve led other Sales staff, working tirelessly along with numerous departments, across many disciplines, to develop and deploy a device that would eliminate this barrier to continued volume growth. With the help of engineers, billing experts, purchasing, and many other departments, work progressed with vendors to develop, test, and then distribute customer automation devices.

The Customer Automation Program eventually outgrew the resources of Sales, growing into what is now a key component of FedEx's business strategy—"Getting Close to the Customer." From these pioneering and near-primitive (by today's standards) technological beginnings, this initiative has expanded to include automated billing, report writing, logistics support, regulatory information, and other important customer support tools. Because of the secure environment created by the permission culture, many key innovations at FedEx started with individuals seeing the need and taking the initiative in developing solutions. There was clear understanding between senior management and the FedEx team that there was only one goal: creating and keeping customers. People were empowered—had permission—to do whatever was needed to develop solutions for customers' logistics and information needs.

Working Outside a Job Description

Looking back on my 22 years at FedEx, some of my most satisfying assignments had nothing to do with responsibilities related to the position I was in at the time. These were assignments that were challenging and helped me grow as a professional—also a result of the permission culture created by my bosses. As Director of Materials and Resource Planning, I saw a way to improve the corporate long-range planning process for hubs and airport facilities. I approached Ken Willoughby, my boss at the time, about exploring this opportunity. He immediately gave his permission. I led a cross-functional team for three months that analyzed the current method and developed a new and streamlined process. Our proposal was well received, and the whole team received recognition from executive management. I learned a lot about the bigger picture at FedEx through my exposure to the total business process. In fact, that assignment led to my next position, Managing Director of System Form Engineering. Jim Barksdale, Ken Willoughby, and other officers were secure. They were not threatened by people with new ideas. They did not need to get credit. They were not worried about failure.

Customer Experience on the Phone

Jim Petrie, Managing Director of Customer Service at FedEx, shared a permission culture story from his department. One of his senior managers saw a way to reduce the amount of time customer service agents had to wait while the customers who called FedEx to schedule a pickup considered the Saturday delivery option.

Before the change, the agent on the phone would ask whether the customer would like the shipment to be delivered Saturday for an additional $10 fee. This would create a lag in time while the customer checked with other people in the organization to see whether they needed the Saturday delivery option. The revised process was to change the question to a statement: "If you'd like Saturday delivery, please mark the airway bill accordingly. There will be a $10 surcharge. Otherwise it will be delivered Monday."

The call was complete, and the wait time was eliminated.

The senior manager got immediate permission to implement the change. Implementation of this idea resulted in improved customer experience, increased agent productivity, and significant cost savings. Jim shared this idea with Sheila Harrell, vice president of planning, in the Customer Service division. She liked the idea and asked her training staff to incorporate the new method in all new hire training and in the updates issued to existing employees nationwide.

During my work with other companies since leaving FedEx, people have told me about creative problem-solving opportunities that were missed in their organization because employees were afraid to express ideas conflicting with management's stated opinion.

For the organizations where this mind-set prevails, the lack of conflict inhibits risk-taking and innovation since people are reluctant to challenge ideas. Much creative energy is wasted by playing it politically safe. In this environment, "group think" becomes the accepted norm for being a team player. I have witnessed numerous meetings where senior executives waited to hear the boss's take on critical business issues and then followed that lead, even if they had concerns or ideas of their own.

> Progress comes from the people who think against the grain. Without nonconformists, you don't advance.
>
> — Saw Ken Wye, Managing Director, Microsoft
> Singapore, *Fast Company*, September 1999

The permission statement can help sustain the innovation culture. A permission statement also reminds managers that their behavior can stifle the expression of creative ideas. As companies grow in size, bureaucracy in the guise of control creeps in. And approval processes and committees can discourage innovation. It is important that organizations be aware of this reality. The key to creating a secure environment for employees to develop and release their creative potential is a strong internalized belief on the managers' part that employees can and should have ideas that are better than those of the management. If managers simply go through the motion of asking for ideas and opinions, employees can sense the lack of sincerity.

Let Employees Know That You Fully Embrace the Potential for Failure as Part of Innovation

Fear of failure is the biggest obstacle to innovation. It is critical that managers communicate the importance of trying new ideas even if occasionally one of them fails. When failures occur, the manager should applaud the initiative and focus on what has been learned instead of casting blame. Once employees realize that their manager is sincere about eliminating the fear of failure, they will be more likely to take risks with innovative ideas.

Throughout its successful innovation and growth journey, FedEx has had its share of failures—some with significant monetary losses. Once it became clear that a particular innovation was not going to produce the expected results, plans were developed to systematically discontinue or modify the proposed process or product.

In the early 1980s, FedEx saw an opportunity to offer same-day facsimile delivery service under the trade name "ZapMail." The concept was that FedEx couriers would pick up a critical document and take it to a location that had a custom-designed Zap-Mail machine, where it would be transmitted to a ZapMail machine in the destination city. Within a matter of hours, a sharp facsimile of the original document would be delivered to the recipient, and the original would be transported and delivered overnight. When this service was in development, good-quality fax machines were not yet being marketed. But by the time ZapMail was implemented, satisfactory fax machines became readily available at affordable prices. FedEx decided to take a big write-off and get out of the ZapMail business. Nobody was fired as a result of this decision. Every employee who participated in developing and implementing ZapMail was given an opportunity to work in the growing express business.

International expansion had become a key part of FedEx's growth strategy. When, in 1991, it became apparent that the domestic (within United Kingdom) and Intra-European business was not going to be profitable, FedEx decided to take a major write-off and got out of that business. As a result, FedEx recorded an operating loss of $105 million, its first quarterly loss since 1978. These failures did not stop FedEx from innovation. In fact, the ongoing international business expansion is one of the key drivers of overall business growth. These are just a few corporate level examples. Many smaller division or department level ideas did not work as expected and were modified or discontinued.

FedEx has a regional hub in Newark, New Jersey. Its design includes automation of the package sorting operation. Every FedEx package has a bar code embedded with the routing information. The sort system design involved scanners that would read the bar code on the package and automated diverters that would push the packages in the slides designated for specific destinations. Scanners were placed to scan the package from top and sides. When employees placed the packages on the conveyor, they made sure that the bar code label side was facing up. The system tested well and was permanently installed. It was expected that a small percentage of packages would not be read by the scanners in the first pass and would have to be recirculated. During the actual operation, it was discovered that the no-read rate was much higher than had been estimated. This happened because packages would tumble on the belt as they traveled from the first floor to the second floor, leaving the bar code label facing down and unreadable by the scanners.

The solution to this problem called for installing scanners to read the packages from the bottom as well. The scanners cost

$200,000. Executive management asked lots of questions and approved the additional expenditure. What is important to note here is that conveyors at FedEx moved at much higher speeds than in typical warehousing operations. The sort system designers knew that they had permission to experiment and adapt new technology that would take FedEx operations to the next level in productivity and service.

Integrate "Leading for Innovation and Balance: A Nurturing Relationship" in Leadership Development

It would be ideal if all humans were taught two basics equally: (1) how to make a living, and (2) how to live a balanced life that reflects one's values and priorities. People learn the basics about a chosen profession through academic studies. Then they get practical hands-on training in the business world. But no one teaches how to live a balanced life. That is something people often have to seek out for themselves.

Leadership is an extension of the whole person, the analytical side and the feeling side—the whole human. Whatever affects the person also affects those leadership abilities. To be the most effective leader, a manager must dare to be as complete a human being as possible. A person celebrates life in its fullness by leading a balanced life. Certainly it is a balancing act that requires thinking in a way that at first is unfamiliar for most people, but the payoff is huge and long-lasting.

Leaders are paid for the quality and creativity of their decisions and the decisions made by their staffs, not for the hours worked. When leaders take time for their personal lives, it helps to develop and release feelings and imagination, the creative side of the brain. People need to give themselves permission to celebrate life in its fullness.

Interpersonal skills (how we deal with others) are directly related to intrapersonal skills (how we deal with ourselves). It is difficult to be sensitive to work/life balance needs of others if we are insensitive to our own balance needs.

Where a person is in life is a cumulative result of all the choices, big and small, a person has made so far. To improve the quality of life and balance in life, we must improve how we make choices.

I was speaking with the vice president of Human Resources of a Fortune 500 company that offers a wide range of work/life benefits. The Human Resources department had just completed an organization-wide survey about the company's benefit programs. A key finding was that employees appreciated the various work/life benefits that the company made available, but they were not comfortable using them because their immediate supervisors did not support or encourage their use. That reluctance reflects a lack of awareness of the direct relationship between employees' work performance and life balance.

The managers had not internalized that their performance is measured by how well their employees do and that the employees' performance reflects the quality of management. The following unwritten employment contract with the new breed of workers illustrates this relationship:

Level 1: I need a job to pay for my basic needs (fulfilling the needs of the body). You give me a job, and I will give you just enough to keep my job.

Level 2: If the job is interesting and challenging (fulfilling the needs of the mind in addition to meeting the basic needs), then I will give to the job much more than the minimum daily requirement.

Level 3: If the job, the organization, and the manager make me feel valued as a person with a life outside the job and provide a sense of meaning and contribution to the community-at-large (fulfilling the needs of the spirit, mind, and body), then I will give you all I have to offer—creativity and commitment.

During my tenure at the FedEx Leadership Institute, I was the team leader for a weeklong leadership development course for newly promoted managing directors. I worked with Thonda Barnes, the course designer and one of the most innovative persons I have ever had the pleasure to work with in the corporate world. Together, we presented the course "Leading for Innovation and Balance: A Nurturing Relationship."

The learning objectives for this module were:

- Understand the mutually supportive relationships between professional and personal effectiveness—leadership excellence and work/life balance.
- Understand how your ability to model and support work/life balance creates a caring environment and enhances your leadership ability to tap discretionary effort—FedEx's competitive edge.
- Develop a personalized action plan addressing the root causes, internal and external, of imbalance in your unique environment.
- Understand the role of leadership and work/life balance in developing the organization's innovation capacity.

All training modules at the Leadership Institute are experientially based. The indoor class was a four-hour module, and the outdoor class was a full-day module. In the indoor class, the module started with the class answering the following four questions in small group breakout sessions.

1. If you had work/life balance what would it look like?
2. What is the impact of work/life imbalance on your personal and professional life?
3. What has stopped you from maintaining work/life balance?
4. What ideas or strategies have you used successfully to restore your work/life balance?

Each group presented their answers to one of the four questions and was asked to discuss all four questions. The chosen spokespersons from each of the four small groups shared their group's findings with the larger group. The other three groups gave input from their discussion if the presenting group had not already covered a particular topic. The class facilitator helped the group understand that by treating work/life balance as optional, they were paying a high price in areas that mattered to them most—relationships, health, and leadership effectiveness.

Building on the responses from the group breakouts, the seminar facilitator presented the model shown in Figure 7.2 for evaluating and making future choices.

This model has the following eight characteristics:

1. Life and the total self have to be regarded, not as collection of isolated components, but as an integrated whole.
2. Career is an important part of life, but just that—a part, not the whole life.
3. The components have to be taken apart from time to time and refitted together.
4. Expansion in one component cannot compensate for a missing component.
5. Only the individual can define the scope and sources of self-fulfillment within each of the four components of the work/life balance circle.

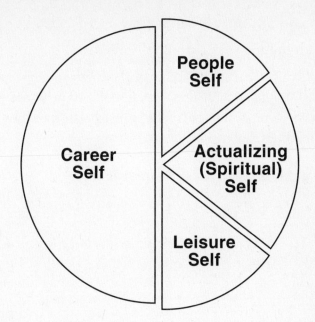

FIGURE 7.2 Work/Life Balance Circle: Celebrating Life in Its Fullness

6. The ceiling to one's personal happiness is set by the component of lowest satisfaction.

7. Each component has its own joys and disappointments and is supportive of others in both success and failure.

8. Each component has elements of others but cannot totally substitute for the others as each component satisfies a specific life need.

The feedback from the participants in the course was positive, with comments such as, "We get so tied up in our day-to-day work pressures and never get a chance to reflect on the bigger picture. This course allowed me to do that." And, "The amount of time devoted to Life Balance was surprising and reassuring. This says a lot about the value the company holds us in."

Practice and Support Balance

Balance on the Job

Managers typically have three areas of responsibilities: technical/operational, managerial, and leadership. To add maximum value as a manager, it is critical to have the proper balance of time and energy among these responsibilities.

Balancing the Three Areas of Responsibilities

At FedEx, all managers can call any managing director, vice president, or senior vice president's office to invite the executive to speak at staff meetings, all-employees meetings, or planning sessions. Although managers sometimes have to adjust the date or time to fit into an officer's schedule, the executives are always cooperative. By their actions, the officers communicate that any opportunity to interact with employees is important and that they will find time to do so.

Dave Bronczek, President and CEO of FedEx Express makes it a point to speak to the newly promoted frontline managers who attend the weeklong Leadership Principles I class. If he is going to be out of town, his office makes sure that one of his senior vice presidents speaks to the class. He stays as long as it takes to answer managers' questions. In fact, there were several times when employees followed him to the parking lot and continued the conversation for another 30 minutes. At the end of the class when the managers fill out the class evaluations, they typically list Bronczek's talk as informative and inspiring, and his visit as the highlight of the week.

As Managing Director of Materials and Resource Planning or System Form Engineering, I had quarterly all-employees meetings. In every meeting, a vice president from one of the eight groups we supported in the company spoke to the group about overall company strategy and the key role our department played in helping them do their jobs better.

Balance between Doing and Thinking

There are times when the entire workday is spent in meetings, leaving no time for thinking. Similarly, employees who are busy *doing* all the time are getting things done, which is important. But they are unlikely to be offering many creative contributions to the organization.

Creative problem solving requires clear thinking to process the information and position the imagination to generate what-ifs. The creative process cannot be rushed. If the mind is constantly busy solving one crisis after another and feels rushed, it is hard to focus on a creative solution to a problem.

The following three practices that evolved over time became part of the FedEx culture. Implementing these practices can help ensure that managers and employees take time out for thinking.

Post-Operation Meetings

No matter what type of business you are engaged in, it is always wise to review your team's activities soon after completion because during the rush of operation everyone is busy getting the job done and not taking much time to think. Karl Birkholz, Vice President of Memphis Hub, holds morning meetings with his management team after the night sort. As a group, they ask, "What went well last night?" and "What did not go well?" This process allows everyone on the team to understand the total operation and to brainstorm ideas to improve future sorts.

One of the ideas that the management team developed early on was *flexible manpower*. At different times of the night, and based on the flight origin city, certain parts of the hub were busier than the others. The director of planning and engineering developed a computer simulation model for a manpower movement plan based on historical data and that day's inbound information. This kind of planning was the key to successfully handling 25 to 38 percent growth in volume while meeting the cost per package goals. Similar meetings, referred to as A.M. or P.M. meetings, took place on a regular basis in all operational areas around the world.

Quality Action Teams

Many organizations form teams to solve problems and continually improve their performance. At FedEx, all levels of management participate in Quality Action Teams (QAT). In fact, for each of the elements of the Service Quality Indicator (SQI), a senior officer is designated to lead the improvement initiative. Under the guidance of the designated senior officer, Quality Action Teams were formed at each level to identify and address the root causes of any problems identified.

Department Planning Sessions

While creative thinking can occur in an office or meeting room, there is something to be said about being close to nature, among trees, by a lake. It relaxes the brain cells to make new connections. It is likely attributable to being away from the e-mails and telephone. Ken Willoughby, vice president in Central Support Services and my boss for several years, had a cabin in the woods by a lake about three hours away from Memphis. Once a year, he took his management team for an all-day planning session at his cabin. The agenda for the planning session was flexible and allowed whatever time was needed for reflection.

Balance Off the Job (Work/Life Balance)

For employees to adopt a balanced life way of thinking, it is important for them to hear the thoughts on the practice from leaders of the organization. They need to hear leaders' personal stories about balancing the dichotomy of work and personal life, and to be reminded that the organization is committed to supporting that balance.

Tracy Schmidt, Chief Financial Officer for FedEx, told employees this anecdote about his life: "The top priorities in my life are faith, family, and work, in that order. To help me lead life in accordance with these priorities and maintain my work/life balance, I've signed a contract with my children. The contract spells out in detail my duties as a father and husband. If I'm not doing the things as spelled out in the contract, I've asked them to hold me accountable and believe me, they do."

During the Leadership and Life Balance course, Friday mornings were reserved for a chat with Fred Smith. During one of these exchanges, a managing director from Hong Kong asked him, "Mr. Smith, in the class we talked about life balance. With all the responsibilities you have, how do you maintain your life balance?" Fred told the class that while FedEx was a big part of his life, it was just that—a part of his life, and not his whole life. At the end of the day, he said, it's a job. He said he has to continually remind himself of that. FedEx picks up and delivers three million packages every day with 24 million scans a day. At all levels of management, it requires lots of energy to run FedEx. He told the group that it takes some physical activity to recharge batteries. So Fred plays tennis regularly. He encouraged employees to have hobbies and other interests and to read books in other fields. "Don't make FedEx your whole life," he said. Fred is an avid reader who regularly sent copies of books and articles that he found interesting to the management team at FedEx.

Provide Flextime and Other Work/Life Benefits

Over the past 30 years, the workforce demographics have changed significantly. More and more women are working out of the home and at the same time taking care of a family at home. Many workers (both dual-career couples and single parents) are the primary caregivers of their aging parents. The traditional family, in which the father works and mother stays home to take care of the children is becoming more often an exception than the norm. It is critical that companies develop flextime options that allow both the company to meet its business needs and help employees to meet their family obligations. Research has shown conclusively that this is not just a nice thing to do but a good business decision as well.

Job Sharing

When employees for personal or family reasons cannot work full time but are interested in working part time, then two employees may be able to share one position. The following example of job sharing in the Human Resource Development (HRD) department shows how it allowed FedEx to keep two qualified professionals.

Shellie Meeks was working full time in HRD when she had her first child. She approached her manager about sharing her job with another person so she could work part time. Karen O'Malley, who also had a new baby, was working part time in the Customer Service call center. She applied for and was offered the part-time position in HRD. Shellie worked Monday, Tuesday, and Wednesday. Karen worked Wednesday, Thursday, and Friday. They continued this arrangement for more than four years. Both had another baby during that period. "Shellie and I both were very grateful to FedEx and did everything, even if that meant working extra hours, to make sure the projects were done on time and were of high quality," said Karen about the arrangement.

Flextime/Part Time

As discussed, FedEx operations work on tight time frames to ensure that packages are picked up and delivered on time. In time-critical functions, employees have to work as scheduled. Other departments use flextime and part-time options based on the work performed in the group.

> Managing human capital effectively is the No. 1 reason successful companies make money, according to new study from consultants Watson Wyatt Worldwide of more than 500 North American companies. Giving employees rewards that are commensurate with their contribution is among the most important HR practices contributing to the bottom line, the study found. Other bottom-line boosting practices include flexible working conditions, strong recruiting of talent, and focused use of technology.
>
> —Executive Briefing, *HR Magazine*, December 2001

For employees to feel comfortable taking advantage of an organization's work/life programs, they must feel the commitment of managers who lead by example. Fred Smith was selected CEO of the year for 2004 by the *Chief Executive* magazine. Editor-in-Chief Bill Holstein interviewed Fred about FedEx and his leadership style. One of the questions that Bill asked was, "On a more personal note, how do you maintain work-life balance?" Fred responded "Well, that's part of the discipline I told you that you have to bring to your job. And anybody who works themselves into exhaustion or incoherence, doesn't have the discipline to do the job to begin with. So I don't take the job home with me, you know, with worry beads or anything like that. I may take some reading home. But I enjoy reading.

"And I have a very great, as you might imagine, full family life. I have grandchildren, I still have children in college, and I have some kids that are athletes. I love to go to their games and watch them, as I have for all of them. I play a lot of tennis, try to get my heart rate up."

Fred has company in the CEO ranks when it comes to leading a balanced life.

When Shelly Lazarus, head of Ogilvy & Mather Worldwide, tells her employees to get a life outside the office, she means it. That's because she sees outside interests and commitments as a sine qua non of O&M's chief asset: creativity. Lazarus once skipped a board meeting in Paris to go on a ski trip with her family. "People were horrified ... (but) you must keep your perspective, it's only business."

> —*Global Literacies* by Robert Rosen, *Fortune*, Best
> Business Books, Anne Fisher, May 15, 2000

Roberto Goizueta was CEO of Coca-Cola from 1981 to 1997. Most afternoons, he left the office around 4:30 P.M. He would ride up front with his driver and listen to country music on the way home, and then spend a quiet evening with his family. During his tenure, Coke's market value increased from $4.3 billion to $181 billion.

Lynn Minton in her column in the Sunday *Parade* magazine, June 2, 2001, issue, posed the following question to teenagers: What song speaks specially to you? A 16-year-old responded, "'Cats in the Cradle' by Harry Chapin (about a dad too busy to spend time with his son) reminds me of my dad and me. I've always wanted a close relationship with him, but I feel he doesn't have enough time for me. One day I won't be there for him, and there he'll be. I love you, Daddy!"

The father in the preceding example knows that he is missing out on the opportunity to build a close relationship with his daughter. This creates inner conflict. The leadership practices and organizational support systems discussed in this chapter can help reduce these conflicts and create secure environment for people to express and accept wild, disruptive, and conflicting creative ideas.

Fear of rejection keeps many people from expressing their ideas. Leaders by their day-to-day behavior can create a secure environment that can help minimize this fear.

Creative thinking takes place in our brains. Just like the heart, the brain needs unclogged arteries to carry fresh blood and oxygen. A balanced life allowing time for play and exercise helps keep arteries clean. Play and hobbies spark imagination and, ultimately, creative thinking.

PRACTICAL IDEAS FOR CREATING A SECURE ENVIRONMENT

- Expect employees to treat everyone inside and outside the company with dignity, respect, and fairness. Institutionalize a confidential way for employees to address any concerns or grievances they may have about the way they are being treated on the job.
- Actively solicit ideas from employees and act on those that are most promising.
- Encourage, acknowledge, and reward divergent thinking and multiple points of view. The best ideas often emerge from constructive conflict.
- Develop and post a Permission statement in all meeting rooms.
- Schedule brown-bag lunchtime discussions about stress management and balance.
- Leaders should schedule activities on their weekly calendar that reflect a balance among their technical, managerial, and leadership responsibilities.
- When announcing that someone has been promoted or assigned to an important project, highlight the person's previous involvement in the generation, acceptance, and implementation of creative ideas.

TABLE 7.1 To Keep Innovating and Outperforming the Competition

Engage employees in the enterprise and create clear expectations for active involvement in the innovation process.	Expect and help employees continually grow their knowledge and skill bases.	Create a secure environment for the expression and acceptance of creative ideas.		
1. Share the company's goals and strategies in simple and plain language.	1. Require employees to update and expand their knowledge and skill bases.	1. Develop and sustain a "Permission culture."		
2. Include employees from all areas and at all levels in creating and keeping customers.	2. Provide resources and put support systems in place.	2. Let employees know that you embrace the potential for failure as part of innovation.		
3. Set measurable goals for improving customer value propositions.	3. Actively participate in learning activities.	3. Integrate "Leading for Innovation and Balance" in leadership development.		
4. Tell employees regularly how they are making a difference.	4. Hold employees accountable for updating their knowledge and skill bases.	4. Practice and support balance.		

- Institute flextime and other work/life balance programs.
- Acknowledge and reinforce calculated risk taking in trying new ideas even if they do not turn out as planned.
- Schedule onsite and off-site social activities that facilitate interaction among employees and across management levels (see Table 7.1).

Chapter 8

Encourage Collaborative Development of Creative Ideas

You don't possess all the wisdom. You must collectively search for the answer.

—Norm Wilcox, Former Managing Director,
FedEx Subic Bay, Philippines

At this point in the innovation and performance culture development, employees are actively involved in improving the business enterprise. They are acquiring updated knowledge and skill bases and are generating what-if ideas. The work environment is conducive to the free flow of creative thought, and managers feel secure accepting those ideas even if they conflict with their stated and preferred approaches to solving the problems.

The fourth leadership responsibility for creating a thriving innovation culture is to encourage collaborative development of raw, creative ideas (see Figure 8.1). Before an idea can be implemented, it must be made palatable to the many people it will affect. The raw idea must be developed before it is ready for implementation.

Depending on the scope, any idea and the resulting change will affect multiple departments in the organization. A business model change will affect every department in the enterprise. A business process change will affect every function involved in that process.

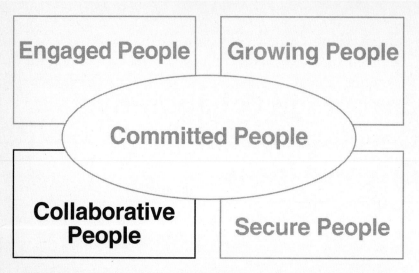

FIGURE 8.1 Innovation and Performance Culture: Fourth Dimension

When you ship an overnight package in the United States through FedEx, it is processed by at least five departments—Domestic Ground Operations pick up and deliver the package, Airport Operations load and unload the airplane, Flight Operations fly the airplane, Sort Operations sort the package in the national or regional hubs, and Information Systems track the package. Any change in one area will affect all the others. Introduction of a new product or service to any of the five departments can also affect other areas including sales, marketing, materials planning, training, maintenance, and human resources.

Complete development and refinement of the raw idea demands active collaboration among all the affected units of the organization. This approach not only ensures that the idea will be fully evaluated and developed, but also positions the company for successful implementation. When people from several departments, varied backgrounds, and different perspectives work together to refine an idea, the finished product is likely to be far better than the result any one of them would have come up with alone.

People who are of a different age, gender, or race literally see things that you miss—and their insights and perspectives help sharpen your own understanding. On the campaign trail, in covering Congress or working on issues such as education or health care, I cannot begin to count the number of times a reporter, very unlike me in background, has noted something or made a comment that caused the light bulb to flash above my bald head.

—David S. Broder, a columnist for the *Washington Post*,
April 7, 2003 column

ENCOURAGE THE COLLABORATIVE DEVELOPMENT OF CREATIVE IDEAS

The following four leadership practices are needed to fulfill this responsibility:

1. Lead by example: Practice collaborative problem solving.
2. Create the needed processes and infrastructure for collaboration.
3. Break down hierarchical and departmental barriers through social activities.
4. Recognize and celebrate teamwork.

Lead by Example: Practice Collaborative Problem Solving

A manager's behavior sets the tone for employees in the department. If they see the manager actively collaborating with peers, the employees will also actively collaborate at their own levels, where the ideas are developed.

The Human Capital Management Program

Kay Coop has held several positions at the managing director level in FedEx's Human Resources department. One of the most enjoyable positions she held was Director of Human Capital Management (HCM). The HCM program was developed when the "Safety Above All" task force set a goal of reducing the number of days injured employees were out on medical leave. The objective was to create a process that created opportunities for employees out on medical leave, to come back to work. This would be a win-win situation because it accommodated the company's need for reducing the number of days employees were absent and the employees' need to be productive in a job that accommodated their current health status.

What Kay enjoyed about her role in this program was achieving active collaboration across the organization to develop and successfully implement the innovative process. The people responsible for this process did not report to Kay. She was the facilitator for the task force.

Before HCM, there was no formal process for dealing with employee health-related issues including the lack of effective training for employees who would be taking on new temporary positions while they recovered from injuries. There was nominal cooperation between the few people who were currently performing this responsibility. There was inconsistency across the organization with potential legal exposure. There were no reliable statistics on lost time, and the injury rate was high.

The first thing the task force did was to involve all the stakeholders in the process. Kay began speaking with her peers in human resources, operations, legal, finance, and executive management about the tremendous opportunity and the current status. The vice presidents in the affected areas saw the opportunity and became actively involved on a steering committee for the project. This support at the vice president level was a key to the program's success. They also assigned managers from their areas to work on the task force. The task force members worked across functions and disciplines to answer the following questions: What worked? What were the barriers? What process do we need to put in place to overcome these barriers? And, how are we going to measure our success? Before proposing the changes in the Medical Absence policy, the task force met with frontline employees in 10 locations to get their input. The HCM manager position was changed from an informal to a formal position, which streamlined and standardized the process. Finally, a training course in the new process was designed for HCM managers.

The changes significantly improved ongoing communication with employees and provided better follow-up with both the employees and vendors contracted to manage the workers' compensation and disability programs. By the time Kay's task force had completed institution of the "Temporary Return-to-Work" program as part of the HCM process, medical leave absence days had been reduced by more than 50 percent. The financial savings were in the tens of millions. Monthly reports were developed for all levels of management.

Each year, FedEx held an annual meeting during which speakers from major divisions shared their HCM success stories. The annual meeting gave Human Capital managers the opportunity to develop relationships among themselves, continue education in the latest issues, evaluate the current status of the program, and identify any needed changes. Smaller meetings were held at the regional level. At these meetings, recognition awards were presented to the top performers in each of the three operating divisions.

Airline Scheduling

Mike Staunton, Vice President of Airline Scheduling, is another FedEx leader who practiced collaborative problem solving on a regular basis. In the express transportation business, flight expenses are a big part of the cost of doing business. One year, during the fiscal year budget development process, senior management noticed that the cost of doing business totaled more than the budget. Mike was asked to reduce the number of flight hours to help bring the overall costs in line with the budget set by the finance department.

He could have simply asked his staff to explore alternatives and make recommendations to reduce the flight hours. But he immediately called the directors of planning functions in the other divisions to collectively brainstorm alternative operating scenarios to reduce flight hours while maintaining FedEx's commitment to 100 percent on-time delivery. In the early days, when FedEx was growing 20 to 40 percent annually and new cities were being opened, there was always a shortage of airplanes. Mike sat down individually with the operations directors in the field, who were going to be responsible for making the schedule work, to discuss options for the integrated flight schedule and operating plans. Everyone had a piece of the puzzle, and they all had to collaborate to make sure the system worked as designed. Many variables had to be taken into account (How many aircraft were available to fly? How many airplanes needed to be allocated as spares and for maintenance?), and they all had to be considered in light of the sales forecast.

Kay and Mike set marvelous examples of bringing people together to generate, refine, and implement innovative solutions.

One person cannot possibly keep up with the details and changes taking place in the various areas of an organization. But a collaborative problem-solving environment brings people together to share the most up-to-date information with others throughout the enterprise. Educating employees about your piece of the puzzle and learning about their pieces of the puzzle makes all the stakeholders knowledgeable about the total business process. This enables them to develop solutions that work for all.

Create the Needed Process and Infrastructure for Collaboration

Networked computers have higher computing power than individual computers. Similarly, linked (collaborating) brains have higher creative thinking power than an individual brain. A thriving innovation culture has built-in processes and an infrastructure to encourage collaboration. Here are a few examples of these processes at FedEx.

Joint Management by Objectives

As discussed in Chapter 5, many companies use a Management by Objectives (MBO) program to align department objectives with corporate strategies and goals. This helps ensure everybody is pulling in the same direction. FedEx has a structured MBO program. The materials planning and maintenance departments used the MBO process successfully to create a collaborative problem-solving environment.

One of the inventories managed by the Materials and Resource Planning group was spare parts for Ground Support Equipment (GSE) that included the equipment for loading and unloading containers on the airplanes and equipment to transport containers to and from the airplanes to sort operations. Ron Schaming was the managing director of the GSE maintenance group, and I was managing director of the Materials and Resource Planning group.

When a mechanic encountered a difficulty in getting the needed spare parts, he would go to his manager and report the problem. The GSE maintenance manager would go to Ron who would call me with the concern. After hearing from Ron, I would call my manager, who would call the analyst to find out what had happened. The analyst would follow up with the mechanics and this loop would start again. At one of the lunches we scheduled each quarter, we both commented that the day-to-day problems were taking too much of our time and we were not adding any value. Most often, the reason the mechanics were not getting the right parts when they came to the parts room window was lack of communication between the maintenance people and the material analysts about preventive maintenance, upgrades, and other planned and unplanned activities.

We agreed that there had to be a better way to address these concerns and that the solution had to come from the people in our respective departments. The key was to create a collaborative environment at every level of the organization. We knew that if key equipment, such as a DC-10 loader, should become inoperable for lack of spare parts, this problem would negatively affect the extremely time-sensitive sort operations. We agreed to develop joint MBOs with measurable goals for material availability and turnaround time on special requests. At FedEx, MBOs were shared from Senior VP down; this aligned everyone within a division. Ron and I were looking to find a way to do this between divisions.

We jointly met with our staffs and shared our MBOs with them. Following our lead, the managers also developed joint MBOs, and the professionals developed joint Performance by Objectives (PBOs). Successful completion of the MBOs and PBOs was a key driver of the performance and variable compensation tied to achieving the corporate People, Service, Profit goals and individual MBOs.

At the director level, we met monthly with all the players to get an update on their progress and ask them how we could help. Together, they came up with several creative solutions to address the lack of communication, including a recommendation that the GSE material analysts set up a satellite office in the GSE parts room. This arrangement helped develop a strong working relationship and vastly improved the communication. The problems were solved at the right level.

This process worked so well that the GSE manager and the Materials Planning manager asked that the Procurement department be involved in the joint MBO process. Because purchase requests from Materials Planning went to the buyers in the Procurement department, who made sure spare parts arrived on time, the buyers were a critical part of the supply chain. Key vendors who supplied the spare parts also became part of the team, and the four parties collaborating together came up with innovative solutions that improved the spare parts availability service level to over 99 percent while substantially reducing FedEx's investment in inventories.

Cross-Functional Teams

Whether your business is large or small, changes are bound to affect people throughout the organization in different ways. By involving them when planning the changes, you get the benefit of their expertise and increase the likelihood that they will enthusiastically support implementation of the changes.

After an idea has been accepted by executive management at FedEx, the sponsoring senior officer sends out a memo to all stakeholders asking them to assign a representative from their areas to work on the idea development team. It is a standard operating procedure, whether it is a new product, an enhancement of existing service, the introduction of new technology, or the tackling of service problems in a specific operational area.

In the early days, new products and services were introduced frequently. That resulted in constant modifications of the five-part airway bill. The airway bill (the document the customer filled out) was used by Operations, Invoicing, Customer Service, and other departments. To make sure every department understood and had input in the redesign, there was an ongoing Airway Bill Committee, a cross-functional team, cochaired by the managing directors of invoicing and information technology.

Every time the airway bill was changed and a new one introduced, the old airway bill inventory had to be written off. The cost of this write-off was approaching six figures. The finance representative raised a concern about the growing write-off and said that the team needed to look into reducing it.

A smaller cross-functional team was formed consisting of representatives from Marketing, Materials Planning, Procurement, the Management Information System group, and the airway bill vendors. Whatever solution the team came up with had to meet three objectives:

1. To maintain FedEx's competitive edge, the solution had to support marketing with introducing the new products or services on a fast-cycle basis.

2. Minimize inventory write-offs.

3. Airway bill availability had to be at 100 percent service level.

The obvious answer to reduce the inventory write-offs was to have minimum inventory on hand at the time of changeover. Inventory levels are driven by several variables, the two key ones being the lead time and the variability of demand. Although the variability in demand created the need for safety stocks, the ideal situation would be a 100 percent accurate forecast and the shortest possible lead time. At that time, the lead time (elapsed time from the receipt of order to delivery to FedEx) from the vendors was eight weeks because of the time it took to get the different color papers from the paper mills. The vendors were not able to stock colored paper in their warehouse because of the unpredictability of the purchase orders from FedEx in terms of timing and quantity. The FedEx buyer was splitting the purchase orders between the various vendors.

By adopting Just-in-Time (JIT) inventory management practices being used in the manufacturing sector at that time, the lead time was reduced from eight weeks to two weeks. Procurement selected two vendors and negotiated a one-year contract with each vendor. The logic behind selecting two vendors versus one was to assure uninterrupted supply in case one vendor had problems. Ongoing information flow both ways was a key feature of these contracts. A rolling forecast for the next 12-month period was provided monthly. This forecast did not authorize the vendors to print airway bills but allowed them to schedule the colored papers from the mills. If for some reason FedEx did not use all the paper, then FedEx would pay for up to one month's storage. This write-off exposure was a fraction of the cost of the finished airway bills.

Break Down Hierarchical and Departmental Barriers (Silos) through Social Activities

For ideas to move from the what-if stage to successful implementation requires cooperation and collaboration across departments and disciplines. Business leaders set the tone for collaborations by their actions. Do they take time to develop deeper relationships with their peers? In staff meetings do they talk negatively about other departments? Do they look for others to blame when something goes wrong? Do they cultivate personal relationships with other groups by getting them together to work as well as play?

It is much easier to collaborate with people you know at a personal level than just as a professional in another department. People feel more secure about expressing what-if ideas in front of managing directors and vice presidents with whom they have shared a drink or a cup of coffee with at interdepartmental functions.

Interdepartmental Picnic and BBQ Contest

Before I moved to Memphis, I had no idea how popular barbecue was in the South. The Logistics department at FedEx took the lead in organizing an annual BBQ picnic and contest. Ken Willoughby, Vice President of Logistics, invited other departments in the company with whom Logistics collaborated to be a part of the picnic. They took this contest seriously. The teams marinated meat overnight and cooked it using secret sauces. They wore elaborate costumes for their skits in the talent competition. It was an all-day picnic that created a fun atmosphere, a perfect backdrop for building relationships with people at all levels of the organization and in other departments.

Creativity flourishes in a relaxed, tension-free environment. To keep a steady pipeline of creative ideas, a leader must ensure that the department and the company are a fun place to work. Laughter refreshes the mind and recharges the batteries. Some managers wrongfully equate a serious work environment with a productive work environment, forgetting that professionals are paid for the quality and creativity of their decisions.

Softball, Basketball, and Golf Leagues

Recreational activities present opportunities for employees from different departments to play together. The relationships built on the playing fields help with the free sharing of ideas and information back on the job.

Every athletic team at FedEx consists of employees ranging from frontline workers to managing directors. The interaction on the court or on the golf course helps break down hierarchical barriers. Many times, the team developing ideas would have trouble getting information from a key department. It was not uncommon for someone on the team to pipe up and say that they knew someone in the department because the person played in the softball league. A telephone call or a meeting between the two would expedite the flow of needed information.

Community Volunteer Programs

FedEx supports and encourages employee participation in community volunteer programs such as Adopt a School. When soliciting funds for the United Way annual campaign, FedEx employees and managers organized an employees' telethon from Memphis. This telethon featuring 49 employee acts from across the continent was broadcast into every FedEx location in America. In addition to the opportunity to work and build relationships with people from other departments and across the country, such events offer the following benefits:

- The satisfaction of making a difference in the city and neighborhoods where the employees live and work.
- Leadership development: 75 FedEx employees worked full-time for a three-month period at United Way as part of their executives-on-loan program.

Officers and Directors Recreational Activities Day

In all my positions—in Logistics or Long Range Operations and Facilities Planning or at the Leadership Institute—I supported operations and people around the world. The annual Officers and Directors meeting, in addition to the presentations and conversations about business strategy, provides opportunities for renewing contacts with peers located around the world. The day before the start of the business meetings was reserved for recreational activities such as golf, tennis, swimming, volleyball, or just sitting by the pool—a perfect opportunity to meet peers in a relaxed setting and put faces on all the e-mails from fellow directors around the world.

Lunches with Peers

The Materials and Resource Planning department supported eight different groups' material needs. We made it a point to invite peer directors and their managers to speak at the all-employees' quarterly planning sessions. I also scheduled lunches with each peer director once a quarter and encouraged my managers to do the same. This made it easier for the managers and professionals in the groups to collaborate and develop innovative solutions at their level instead of elevating every problem to the director level.

Recognize and Celebrate Teamwork in Developing Ideas

All people have a psychological need to feel that their work matters and that they matter. Whether a person is 5 years old or 50 years old, positive reinforcement encourages learners to repeat a behavior. With a greater part of life and energy devoted to work, recognition of one's work by the boss and the organization provides a psychological boost.

An organization's reward system defines its culture. If the company needs collaboration across business units but all its reward systems are based on individual performance, these reward and recognition systems are reinforcing competition, not collaboration. There is a place for individual recognition of employees who perform above and beyond the call of duty, but collaborative development of innovative ideas must also be recognized.

A reward system that encourages collaboration across business units should start at the top and have performance metrics for the enterprise that cut across all business units. Senior management's attitude and orientation determine the attitude and priorities of the people below them.

To recognize superior performance, FedEx has a program called "Bravo Zulu." A Bravo Zulu flag's sticker is put on the memo or plaques issued to employees in recognition of their efforts. (In the U.S. Navy, the Bravo Zulu means "well done.") Managers have the option of including monetary awards with the Bravo Zulu.

After the great success with implementation of the Just-in-Time program for the airway bills, Fred Smith awarded the Bravo Zulu to the JIT team for their work. The program was expanded to include other high-volume Stock Keeping Units (SKU) stored in the warehouse.

FedEx
INTER-OFFICE MEMORANDUM
DATE: August 8, 1985   TO: JIT Team
FROM: Frederick W. Smith

SUBJECT: Just-In-Time Program Implementation at FedEx

I want to extend my heartfelt "BRAVO ZULU" to you for successful implementation of the Just-In-Time material management philosophy at FedEx. As you are aware, development and expansion of our international business demands creative ways of managing the base business. Programs like Just-In-Time, which improve customer service and at the same time reduce investment in inventories, are the keys to maintaining our competitive edge.

Your work on the JIT Team, which crosses divisional lines, exemplifies the team work and total cooperation in action. Thank you for the fine efforts and keep up the good work!

Fredrick W. Smith

The following Bravo Zulu was awarded by Jack Roberts, Vice President and Controller, for the collaborative work in developing and implementing the Joint MBO program.

FedEx
INTER-OFFICE MEMORANDUM
DATE: August 24, 1989   TO: Glenn Chambers
                                             Madan Birla

FROM: W. Jack Roberts cc: CFO

SUBJECT: Appreciation

The Quality Success Story concerning *joint objectives* between Materials & Resource Requirements Planning and Procurement exemplifies the quality process in action. The two of you were instrumental in causing this significant improvement in the working relationship between the two groups.

Thanks for your efforts. Bravo Zulu!

W. Jack Roberts

Glenn and I brought our groups together for a pizza party to celebrate this recognition and to convey our feelings of appreciation for their hard work and collaboration.

It is not uncommon to see managers cooking hamburgers on the grill in the parking lot at FedEx locations around the country in appreciation for their employees' teamwork.

The March 17, 2003, *BusinessWeek* cover story on IBM offered an example of leading by example and recognizing teamwork. In his first board meeting, CEO Samuel J. Palmisano asked the board to put a significant portion of his 2003 bonus into a pool of money to be shared by about 20 top executives for their performance as a team.

Practical Ideas for Encouraging Collaboration

- Even if you do not have a formal MBO program, establish joint performance objectives with your peers in other departments that serve the same customers.
- Schedule occasional lunches with your peers and encourage your staff to do the same.
- Plan joint social activities with other work groups.
- When work groups are not cooperating with each other, focus on rectifying the situation instead of casting blame.

TABLE 8.1 To Keep Innovating and Outperforming the Competition

Engage employees in the enterprise and create clear expectations for active involvement in the innovation process.	Expect and help employees continually grow their knowledge and skill bases.	Create a secure environment for the expression and acceptance of creative ideas.	Encourage collaborative development of raw, creative ideas.	
1. Share the company's goals and strategies in simple and plain language.	1. Require employees to update and expand their knowledge and skill bases.	1. Develop and sustain a "Permission culture."	1. Lead by example: Practice collaborative problem solving.	
2. Include employees from all areas and at all levels in creating and keeping customers.	2. Provide resources and put support systems in place.	2. Let employees know that you embrace the potential for failure as part of innovation.	2. Create the needed processes and infrastructure for collaboration.	
3. Set measurable goals for improving customer value propositions.	3. Actively participate in learning activities.	3. Integrate "Leading for Innovation and Balance" in leadership development.	3. Break down hierarchical and departmental barriers through social activities.	
4. Tell employees regularly how they are making a difference.	4. Hold employees accountable for updating their knowledge and skill bases.	4. Practice and support balance.	4. Recognize and reward teamwork.	

- Create collaboration awards and ask your employees to nominate people from other work groups who have collaborated with them in the development of ideas.
- Whenever possible, encourage members of your work group to work part of the time in departments that are collaborating with your team. Invite members of those work groups to work onsite with your team.
- Develop compensation packages that reward cooperation between individuals and work groups (see Table 8.1).

Chapter 9

Tap Employees' Commitment

I firmly believe that employee dedication mirrors the extent to which an organization demonstrates its commitment to its people. When people know what is expected of them, understand that outstanding performance is rewarded and believe they can make a difference because they will be listened to and are allowed to put their ideas to work, they will make a difference.

Fred Smith, Founder & CEO, FedEx

In a successful innovative and performance culture, employees are engaged in the business enterprise. They are continually updating their knowledge and skill bases. Using their expanded knowledge, new skills, and the power of their imagination, they are generating ideas to improve the customer experience, operational efficiencies, and the company's customer value propositions. They are secure in expressing these ideas. Managers are secure enough to consider the ideas. Employees are working collaboratively to develop the raw, creative ideas.

If one of those ideas is ready to be implemented, and if it is a genuine innovation, it will involve change. Since change takes people out of their comfort zone and disrupts their routine, it often meets resistance. But it does not need to be that way. Change is

173

more likely to be accepted if those affected by it have a say in its implementation and if there is commitment to, and trust in, the organization. How do leaders inspire dedication and tap into this commitment? The leadership responsibilities and corresponding leadership practices, discussed in Chapters 5 through 8, will take care of 80 percent of the work by helping employees feel they are:

- Part of a winning team that's going somewhere
- Continually growing and challenged
- Secure in expressing ideas
- Working for an organization that cares about them as people with interests and obligations outside work
- Part of a group where everyone is eager to collaborate

This chapter discusses the leadership practices for meeting the remaining 20 percent of the needs (see Figure 9.1). Committed

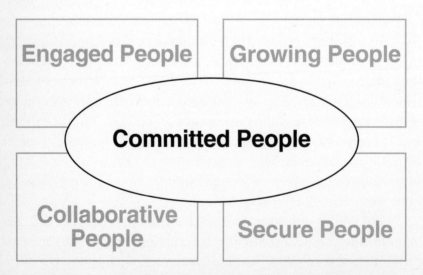

FIGURE 9.1   Innovation and Performance Culture: Fifth Dimension

employees (mind/heart) give their manager the benefit of the doubt even if they do not fully understand the details and benefits of the planned change initiative. Committed employees can be expected to:

- Go beyond formal job descriptions in ensuring successful implementation of the creative ideas.
- Go an extra mile to satisfy the customer.
- Put organization's interest and goals above self-interest.

Gloria Sangster-Fort told me a story about her experience in FedEx's Sales department. FedEx was just starting to offer international express service. She approached a Fortune 100 company that was international in scope, for handling their international shipments. They asked for references. At that time, FedEx did not really have any big clients that were shipping international with other functions added that are generally handled by a freight forwarder.

Gloria was talking to Frank Newman, a colleague at FedEx, about her dilemma in trying to sign up this large account for FedEx's international service. Frank was not part of the Sales organization but had experience in writing operational plans and working internationally. He volunteered to help her develop a proposal. He mapped the process and developed a detailed FedEx solution to handle the business in the three targeted European countries. This plan showed how FedEx would streamline the shipping process and substantially improve the service.

It took two weeks of dedicated effort on Frank's part to develop this comprehensive proposal. Frank had no stake in or direct responsibility for getting this customer's international business, nor did he anticipate any personal gain. But, he was totally committed to FedEx and was willing to do whatever it took to help FedEx grow. Based on this proposal, Gloria was able to secure the account and the first-ever $10 million contract. To show their appreciation for this above-and-beyond effort, Sales awarded him a handsome Bravo Zulu letter and check. The letter was later displayed. Based on this successful experience, Sales created a model for working with other large companies.

Frank's commitment was not forgotten. In fact, he was later hired into Sales and became a managing director. Frank had become known for being innovative and customer centric because of a deed that he did not have to perform.

When Gloria involved Frank in getting her potential customer's business, she was demonstrating the fifth leadership responsibility to build and sustain an innovation culture.

TAP EMPLOYEES' COMMITMENT FOR SUCCESSFUL IMPLEMENTATION OF THE DEVELOPED IDEAS

The following leadership practices achieve this result:

- Build mutually trusting relationships.
- Involve employees in the development of implementation plans.
- Listen to understand instead of listening to respond.
- Let appreciation flow from the heart.

Build Mutually Trusting Relationships

You can use your authority or positional power to get employees to comply with directives. But if you expect them to keep generating, developing, and implementing new ideas—the essence of discretionary effort—the organization and the management must meet their needs. Managers have to be open, honest, caring, and consistent. Those qualities are the keys to personal power and the building blocks for establishing the mutually trusting relationships that are essential for nurturing creativity and commitment.

One cold, blustery night many years ago, a young managing director earned the trust of his team by demonstrating those qualities under extreme pressure. Although Memphis winters are not usually cold and snowy, occasional ice storms can wreak havoc. Consequently, FedEx's Memphis hub has a well-developed contingency plan for deicing airplanes to minimize delays.

This particular night, Linda Wolowicz, who was the Senior Manager of Global Operations Control (GOC), FedEx's command center in Memphis for monitoring and controlling aircraft, received a call from the manager on duty at 4 A.M. informing her that a terrible ice storm was approaching. He predicted that it would prevent FedEx from launching most of its flights on time and cause service failures around the world. At 4:30 A.M. she called Ken May, the young Director of Operations, to inform him of the situation. By 6 A.M. only five aircraft had taken off as opposed to the normal 150 departures. It was obvious that the ice storm contingency plan had not worked.

Following the debacle, Fred Smith, called a special meeting to get to the bottom of the problem. He asked Ken to chair the meeting and make the key presentation. To prepare for it, Ken met with managers from GOC, Flight Operations, Hub Operations, Maintenance, and other departments responsible for executing the deicing contingency plan. He asked everyone to tell him what happened and what they would do to be ready for the next ice storm.

When the big meeting was held, the heads of the departments responsible for executing the contingency plan were ready to present their sides of the story and defend their actions. But they never had to say a word because when Ken started his presentation, he said, "I take full responsibility for what happened." He did not point fingers at anyone even though there was plenty of blame to go around. After presenting a brief analysis of what had happened, he spent most of the time detailing what the team had learned from the experience and what they were going to do to get it right the next time. While executive management was unhappy with the flight delays that had occurred, it was pleased with the analysis and approved the recommendations.

Ken earned the trust and commitment of everyone in the room by the way he handled this incident. Every manager had come to the meeting feeling anxious and expecting to be chastised. But when it was over, they all felt that they were members of an energized team committed to working together to implement Ken's plan, which was really a synthesis of everyone's recommendations.

Henry Bartosch, a former Managing Director of Hub Operations in Memphis, told me about another set of mutually supportive relationships he observed at FedEx. Paula Rankins, one of his senior managers, had a great relationship with her employees. They freely approached her to share their concerns and ideas. When they entered Paula's office, she gave them her full attention. Bartosch noticed that employees would walk into Paula's office to tell her when they had finished a project and offer to help complete other projects. Her entire group had a can-do attitude best illustrated by this story Henry shared with me:

> One hot and humid August night, a hub engineer told me and my senior managers that he had come up with a way to sort documents with significantly fewer people. This was before faxes and e-mails had become ubiquitous, so anything we could do to handle the torrent of documents more efficiently was worth considering. Paula and her managers were the first ones to accept the challenge. They evaluated the proposal, determined that it was doable, and developed a detailed implementation plan. By mid-October, the new process was working and saving

the company money. All this happened because one engineer kept asking "What if?" and one senior manager had developed such trusting and committed relationships with her team that they would do just about anything to get the job done better or more efficiently.

Involve Employees in Developing Implementation Plans

Involvement in developing an implementation plan is empowering. The more involved people are, the more committed they become to its success. While including all affected employees is ideal, it is not always possible. Commitment is still possible, however, by involving representatives of the affected work groups who can keep teammates informed and pass along suggestions and concerns. Expecting every employee to participate in the innovation process goes a long way toward creating the right environment to develop and implement ideas.

The expectation for positive, can-do leadership and involvement has helped FedEx implement many strategic changes on a fast-cycle basis. These changes were keys to maintaining a competitive edge and gaining market share.

In 1982, one of those changes involved meeting customers' needs for earlier deliveries. At the time, FedEx guaranteed overnight delivery by noon the next day. Since express customers usually want the latest possible pickups and the earliest possible deliveries, Marketing proposed that we move up our delivery commitment to 10:30 A.M. This would require extensive changes in all operating divisions. Once we got the green light, we assembled a team consisting of people from all the affected areas to develop implementation plans.

The team met weekly to review progress, concerns, and suggestions for resolving outstanding issues. Between meetings, team members reported the results of their deliberations to their colleagues and solicited additional input.

This systemwide change was successfully implemented in just six weeks, although the team continued to meet for another four weeks to review progress and tweak the operating plan. While they were meeting, who knows how many other teams were meeting to make life better for our customers, our employees, and our shareholders?

Assembling cross-functional teams has become the standard procedure for developing implementation plans throughout the company. Smaller working teams focus on operational details and present them to the larger group at the weekly team meetings. Senior management attends the large team meetings where decisions are finalized on the spot. This allows the implementation team to stay on track instead of being bogged down in bureaucracy.

As companies grow and more layers get added to the management structure, implementation requires more, not less, involvement from senior management. Without someone monitoring and guiding the process from a broader business perspective and making decisions on a timely basis, good ideas can get lost in turf battles between groups that should be cooperating instead of competing with each other.

As Figure 9.2 shows, another significant benefit comes from involving employees at all levels in the development of plans: They usually make valuable contributions as the idea is being considered, developed, and implemented. Throughout the process, there are plenty of opportunities for employees to exercise their creativity and initiative.

Often the employees who actually do the work and are responsible for implementing changes can anticipate potential problems and their solutions better than the idea generators who tend to be focused on the big picture—a step or more away from the action.

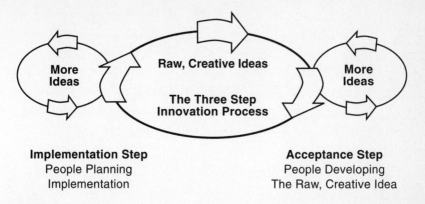

FIGURE 9.2   Ongoing Innovation during the Acceptance and Implementation Steps

Implementation Team Saves over $500,000

Because FedEx's Memphis hub is the linchpin of the vast air-ground network connecting a multitude of U.S. and international cities with each other, every night over a million packages are sorted and processed there. The sorting system is automated. The package scanners read the bar codes on the packages and sort the packages to the designated conveyors. During the automated system design, it was assumed that a very small percentage of the packages, for various reasons, would not be successfully sorted. Two rework slides, East and West, were designed and built into the system. At the rework slides, the packages are inspected manually; if necessary, a new bar code label is applied, and the package is inducted back into the sorting system.

A few years back, the number of packages on the reject slides increased substantially. Per Kewal Gupta, Manager of Sort Systems Conceptual Design, the solution developed by his group was to expand both the East and West slides at a cost of $1.3 million. The concept and the budget were approved, and the implementation team was assembled. During the implementation planning process, an engineer from the Systems and Electrical Engineering group suggested, "What if we scan the package a second time before sending it to the rework slide?" Following up on this idea, the implementation team explored several options including increasing the number of scanners. The implementation team settled on a plan that involved sending rejected packages to the recirculation belt for rescanning using the existing scanners. This procedure reduced the number of no-reads by 80 percent. Expansion of one slide, instead of the two in the original solution, was sufficient to handle the remaining 20 percent. This solution saved more than $500,000 from the original budget of $1.3 million.

Involving Vendors in the Implementation Process

Before Roger Albee came to work for FedEx, he was an account executive at NCR, which supplied some of FedEx's airbills (the documents customers fill out when they ship with FedEx). Part of his job involved serving on a team to help FedEx apply bar codes to the airbills. The team consisted of FedEx engineers and managers as well as representatives of various vendors, including the providers of the airbills, the paper they were printed on, the scanner, and the bar code printer. As the project was nearing completion, the whole team was invited to Memphis to observe a test of the first batch of bar coded airbills.

Before the test began, Albee and his fellow-team members were given a tour of the Memphis hub that can be an awesome experience for anyone who has never seen the size and scope of the operation. Recently, Albee recalled the tour and especially the person who conducted it. He said, "The FedEx manager who conducted the tour had injured his back in a very serious sports accident. He was wearing a heavy back brace and was obviously in pain. I said to myself if there are people like him who are so committed that they would come to work in this condition, I want to work for this company." That's when he decided to leave NCR and join FedEx.

The plane with the test packages arrived and just when the packages were being unloaded, a downpour began. The first thing everyone noticed was that the ink used for printing the bar code started to run. "That told us that we need to use water repellent ink. The plane was rolled into the nearby hanger and we continued the test."

Listening to Understand instead of Listening to Respond

Employees who feel they are being treated with dignity and respect by their managers tend to give their full commitment to them. By listening to understand instead of listening to respond, managers show respect for employees and their ideas. To do this, we need to watch our mind when somebody is talking. Is it busy thinking about what to say in response or is it really trying to understand what the other person is saying? When presented with a problem, managers instinctively try to solve it. Most of the time, however, employees just want the manager to understand the situation they are facing and are not looking for the manager to solve it for them.

That is the situation Jack Roberts was in when FedEx acquired Gelco Express International in 1986 to expand its international business. Jack, who was Vice President and Controller at the time, recalled one of the ramifications of the acquisition: "All of a sudden we had operations all over the world in addition to our U.S. business which had just hit the one billion dollar mark. Unfortunately, it was taking up to eight days to close the books each month and produce financial reports for executive management which wanted them the day after the month ended."

Because Jack's department was struggling to meet this objective, he asked his team to come up with a plan that would reduce the book closing time by half. He told them that he would be available whenever they needed him. Then he got out of their way. The team met regularly to brainstorm ideas that would enable them to close the books in the allotted time.

When the team came up with an idea, they would approach Jack to get his input. His focus during these sessions was to make sure he understood their ideas completely before offering his suggestions because they were coming up with innovative approaches that were very different from the previous system. He saw his role as a coach and encouraged his team to continue developing their ideas. It took them 18 months to develop, test, and fully implement the new closing process, which turned out to be a huge success.

The resulting monthly Corporate Performance Report included more than just how well FedEx did compared with its projections. It analyzed the root causes of variances. It contained detailed analyses right down to the divisional level. It provided customer and productivity data. It even presented a future outlook; that is, if a trend showed a certain expense category was heading in the wrong direction, it was highlighted. Executive management used this report not only to monitor corporate performance but to make important decisions about the allocation of resources.

Accountants responsible for the specific sections of the report took ownership of the new process and proudly put their names on the relevant pages so they could be contacted if anyone had a question regarding the information and analysis. They developed close working relationships with their peers in Operations to continually enhance the information flow and the process.

Executive management was pleased with the results and recognized Jack's staff for their initiative and creative ideas. His role as a leader throughout this process was to make sure his people, who were doing the real work and had the expertise to improve the process, felt that they and their ideas were being understood and supported.

As Jack's story illustrates, listening to understand helps us:

- Encourage the generation of new ideas.
- Genuinely understand other people's ideas.
- Provide feedback based on our understanding.
- Satisfy our employees' need to be understood.

Easier Said Than Done

If listening to understand is so beneficial, why don't we do it more often? To answer that question, we have to consider what it entails. Listening to understand, sometimes referred to as *empathic listening*, means getting out of our own head and into the head of another person. It also involves sensing what is in another person's heart. To do that, we have to pay attention not just to what the other person is saying but *how* he or she is saying it. This includes noting vocal tone, volume, and pitch as well as facial expressions, gestures, posture, and body language. It is an awful lot to ask of us because we tend to be self-centered and focused on our own needs and interests. That is why FedEx encourages its managers, all of whom are considered leaders, to be as selfless as is humanly possible.

Even before management candidates become frontline managers, they are taught that the employees who will be reporting to them will not be working for them. On the contrary, as managers they will be working for the employees. To get that point across, candidates are urged to think about FedEx's organizational structure as an inverted pyramid. The most important people are the many employees on top who directly serve customers. Managers support them, making sure they have the knowledge, skills, and resources they need to deliver impeccable customer service. Each successive layer of management supports the layer above it down to the CEO who supports the entire enterprise.

The inverted pyramid metaphor is not perfect. Managers can and do make decisions that employees may not like. They tend to make more money, too. But it illustrates that selfless, servant leadership is a fundamental value at FedEx. Managers must constantly subordinate their own interests for the good of their employees and the organization as a whole. Although they must hold their employees accountable to do their jobs, they, too, are held accountable by their employees, who evaluate them in an annual leadership survey.

Managers at FedEx must consistently receive good ratings from their employees to be considered effective leaders and to hold their jobs. One item on the survey, "My manager listens to my concerns," speaks directly to the notion of listening to understand. Managers are not just expected to be good listeners. They are actually held accountable for it.

Sometimes a simple adjustment in the language that managers use with employees can make all the difference in the world. When a manager tells an employee that an idea will not work, it is discouraging. In my department, we used something I called the "Power of Positive Speaking." That meant listening to ideas with an open mind and instead of saying why they would not work, complimenting the person for sharing the idea, and asking clarifying questions about the issues that raised a red flag.

Let Appreciation Flow from the Heart

Employees have a need to be recognized for the quality and creativity of their work. A plaque, a letter, a pin, a cup, or a check are great and are appreciated. But recognition means much more if it comes from the presenter's heart. A smile, a kind word, a handwritten note, an honest compliment—all connect at the heart level and thus tap into employees' commitment.

Business is more about emotions than most businesspeople care to admit. It's time to put the passion for work and the joy of creation back into business.

—Daniel Kahneman, 2002 Nobel Prize winner for Economics, quoted in *Fast Company*, January 2003

Gloria Sangster-Fort, Managing Director in Sales at FedEx received many awards during her 20-year career at FedEx. But the one she cherishes the most is a brief handwritten note from Fred Smith after she secured Du Pont's international business. During my career at FedEx, I received multiple awards. But the ones I remember and cherish the most did not involve plaques or checks. They were heartfelt phone calls and notes.

In 1990, one of those phone calls involved the small part I played in helping FedEx become the first service company to win the Malcolm Baldrige Quality Award. As part of the evaluation process, the examiners interviewed me about the strategic planning process at FedEx. I spent three hours doing my best to answer their questions.

When Jim Barksdale called me the next morning, I was a little nervous. Apparently, the night before the examiners had briefed executive management about their interviews that day. To my pleasant surprise and relief, Jim said they were very impressed by the strategic planning process I had described. He just wanted to thank me for doing such a good job. This brief phone call made me feel great for weeks. That Jim had made a mental note of my contribution during the briefing and then had taken the time from his busy schedule to call me first thing in the morning spoke volumes. I felt in my heart that Jim cared about my contribution and about me as a person.

Another FedEx executive who made me feel appreciated is Lenny Feiler, my boss for several years. I always looked forward to coming to work each day to check my in-basket for the handwritten notes of appreciation Lenny would scribble on the memos my staff or I had sent out a few days earlier.

Employees' commitment is the key to successful implementation of creative ideas and outperforming the competition. It is the implementation step that converts ideas into innovation.

Tapping Employees' Creativity and Commitment around the Globe

In the United States.   When FedEx began doing business around the world, especially in countries with value systems quite different from Western norms, supposed experts warned executive management not to try to export its People, Service, Profit (PSP) philosophy, which had been instrumental in tapping employees' commitment and discretionary effort. Those experts said that treating employees with dignity and respect is well and good and involving employees in decisions that affect them is a noble idea. But those ideas will not work in more traditional, hierarchical societies where people expect the boss to have all the answers and make all the decisions. What is more, these experts claimed that in lands where unemployment is rampant, people will put up with anything to keep a job.

To its credit, executive management realized that PSP was not an esoteric philosophy with limited applicability. On the contrary, as the previous examples show, it is as close as one can get to a universal law of human behavior and business success. When a company treats employees well, they are more inclined to treat customers well, which in turn results in greater profitability and higher incomes for everyone involved. Sure, it is necessary to tweak the way the philosophy is applied so that it is compatible with local norms, but FedEx's PSP philosophy has been equally effective in tapping employees' commitment and discretionary effort in different cultures around the world.

At a recent FedEx Retiree Club's monthly lunch meeting in Memphis, a senior pilot who had joined FedEx in the early days shared a story that illustrated the commitment many FedEx employees have to the company and to its customers. He was in Albuquerque and had just closed the plane doors after the ramp agents had finished loading the packages. He was getting ready to start the preflight checks when he noticed a man standing on the other side of the fence waving a small package. He asked the ground crew to get the package, opened the pilot's window, and took it. He put the package in the back and flew it to Memphis for processing and delivering the next day. "That's what you did," he said.

In the United States and Kenya.   It was a harried day in August 1997 when an American plastic surgeon called the FedEx Pearl River, New York, office in desperation. The surgeon, who heads a nonprofit charity called Share, needed the cancer-fighting drug Cytoxan to help Kenyan children under her care. "I knew we had to do something," said Maureen Boylan, a senior invoicing specialist in Pearl River, near Share headquarters. She appointed herself to go to Share's offices, where she picked up the six packages and completed the extensive paperwork required by the Kenyan government. Before heading out, she got approval for FedEx to donate the shipment. When Boylan discovered that civil unrest had caused the FedEx affiliate to close temporarily, she made more calls. "We were able to notify them that the shipment was there, and they made the delivery."

In Australia.   Australia was gearing up for the 2000 Summer Olympics. The traffic restrictions in the city were going to shut down FedEx's pickup and delivery operations. There would be no parking on the streets during normal delivery hours. The FedEx team in Australia sent out a questionnaire to business customers asking whether they would be open. If they were going to be open, the questionnaire asked when and how FedEx could serve their needs during the Olympics.

TABLE 9.1 To Keep Innovating and Outperforming the Competition

Engage employees in the enterprise and create clear expectations for active involvement in the innovation process.	Expect and help employees continually grow their knowledge and skill bases.	Create a secure environment for the expression and acceptance of creative ideas.	Encourage collaborative development of raw, creative ideas.	Top employees' commitment to successfully implement the developed ideas.
1. Share the company's goals and strategies in simple and plain language.	1. Require employees to update and expand their knowledge and skill bases.	1. Develop and sustain a "Permission culture."	1. Lead by example: Practice collaborative problem solving.	1. Build mutually trusting relationships.
2. Include employees from all areas and at all levels in creating and keeping customers.	2. Provide resources and put support systems in place.	2. Let employees know that you embrace the potential for failure as part of innovation.	2. Create the needed processes and infrastructure for collaboration.	2. Involve employees in the development of implementation plans.
3. Set measurable goals for improving customer value propositions.	3. Actively participate in learning activities.	3. Integrate "Leading for Innovation and Balance" in leadership development.	3. Break down hierarchical and departmental barriers through social activities.	3. Listen to understand instead of listening to respond.
4. Tell employees regularly how they are making a difference.	4. Hold employees accountable for updating their knowledge and skill bases.	4. Practice and support balance.	4. Recognize and reward teamwork.	4. Let appreciation flow from the heart.

Some customers were going to be opening earlier so they could receive deliveries then. For the rest, the team devised a plan to have multiple couriers in one vehicle. FedEx delivery trucks would circle the area, and the extra couriers would deliver the packages while the trucks kept moving. FedEx customers were delighted.

PRACTICAL IDEAS FOR TAPPING EMPLOYEES' COMMITMENT

- In group settings, earn employees' trust by focusing on solutions for the future rather than casting blame for past problems.

- Keep an open door, and when employees enter, give them your full attention instead of glancing at e-mail, picking up the phone, and so on.

- Exhibit a contagious can-do attitude.

- Give employees opportunities to be part of cross-functional teams.

- Replace "it won't work" with "that's an interesting idea; help me understand it better."

- In addition to formal recognition memos, plaques, and awards, praise and thank people over the phone, with a handwritten note, or with a pat on the back.

- Empower employees to do whatever it takes, within reason, to satisfy customers (see Table 9.1 on page 190).

Conclusion: Continuing to Lead the Way

At FedEx, leading the way comes naturally. We originated the modern air/ground express industry. We invented the concept of time-critical expedited delivery. We were the first to use bar code labeling in the ground transportation industry and the first express company to offer time-definite freight service.

And yet, today, FedEx is so much more. More services. More technology. All backed by more than 214,000 employees and contractors who are more focused than ever on meeting customer needs—about five million times a day.

As today's FedEx, we're proud to be one of the world's most admired companies. We're proud to be recognized as a great place to work. Most of all, we're proud to continue leading the way for our customers, our investors, our employees, and our communities.

—FedEx 2002 Annual Report

The key to FedEx's continuing leadership has been its employees' understanding and application of the following principles, discussed and illustrated throughout this book:

- Business models, strategies, and processes must be continually evaluated and enhanced to take advantage of changes in the business environment, particularly customers' needs, desires, and expectations.
- In today's highly competitive, global economy, maintaining the status quo is not enough. We must change to grow.

- Growth comes from anticipating and meeting changing customer needs in a competitively differentiated way. Competitive differentiation comes from designing and delivering customer value propositions that are superior to those of competitors and that appeal to both the head and heart.
- Every department and every employee is directly or indirectly involved in designing and delivering customer value propositions.
- All innovations must be customer and market driven.
- While you need an occasional disruptive innovation to stay ahead of the competition, a series of small, incremental innovations can have a huge, cumulative effect on market share and profitability.
- Quarterly earnings are the score. Unique processes, value propositions, capabilities, and market positioning—all products of innovative thinking—determine the score.
- It does not matter whether you are in a manufacturing or a service business; every company is in the customer experience and relationship business.
- Innovation does not just happen. It must be actively supported and managed.
- Innovation is a people process.
  - Everyone must believe that whatever they are doing today can be done better tomorrow.
  - Leaders at all levels inspire others to become actively involved in generating, accepting, and implementing creative ideas (see Figure C.1).

That last principle cannot be overemphasized. When people ask me how Fred Smith built such a great company, I tell them what Fred always says, "It is the FedEx people—the entire team—who are responsible for the company's phenomenal success." He reminds employees of this critical fact at every gathering. It is the

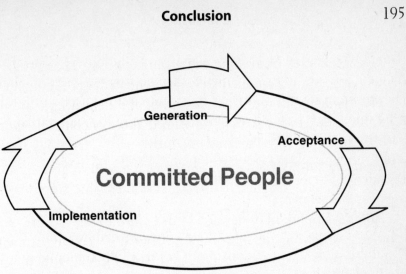

FIGURE C.1   The Three-Step Innovation Process: A People Process

people who took FedEx from an idea in Fred's term paper at Yale to one of the most admired companies in the world. They built and sustained the culture that enables FedEx to keep innovating and outperforming the competition.

What are the elements of this culture? Why do FedEx people "bleed purple?" Why do they do "absolutely, positively whatever it takes" to deliver the goods for all stakeholders?

First of all, one cannot discount the importance of having a truly great, visionary leader who inspires employees to go above and beyond the call of duty. Then there is being part of a highly successful enterprise that has actually changed the way the world does business. Employees are engaged in that enterprise every day because they believe that they are making a difference. As the company attracts new customers, employees see more of their vehicles on the road, more of their planes in the air, more packages flowing through the system, and more opportunities for themselves.

That is why as FedEx has grown, so have its people. The company has always followed a promotion-from-within policy. Many people who started as package handlers in the hub or couriers in the field are now in management, engineering, sales, and so on. In fact, several of FedEx's highest level executives started out on the front line. Dave Rebholz is a great example of this. He started as a part-time clerk in Milwaukee, Wisconsin, in 1976 washing trucks and running packages out to the plane. He is now Executive Vice President of Operations and Systems Support responsible for leading over 80,000 people.

Another important dimension of this culture is the secure environment, which encourages employees to keep coming up with new ideas and makes managers accountable for taking them seriously. Managers do not just listen to their employees. They actively solicit their input, especially when the matter at hand directly affects the employees or their customers. Company policies and performance measurement systems support this behavior.

The next dimension of an innovation and performance culture is the collaborative spirit that inhabits its people. At FedEx, if you call someone across the country or around the world about a problem you cannot solve, you have automatically involved another person to work on it with you. That is why cross-functional teams do such a wonderful job exploring and developing the promising ideas that pay off handsomely so much of the time.

The final dimension of this culture is the commitment of employees that managers tap to implement fully developed ideas. This commitment is exemplified by the service agent who stays late to take care of customers who arrive at the last minute with incomplete paperwork for shipping an international package, the courier who goes out of her way to find a customer even when the address on the package is wrong, or the package handler who walks to work in the middle of the night during a blinding snowstorm. These are the people you can count on when you introduce a new product or service because they are willing to give you their discretionary effort even when it takes them out of their comfort zone and disrupts their routines.

This culture and that discretionary effort enable FedEx to deliver for its customers, its employees, its shareholders, and the community. Customers gain peace of mind as the company partners with them to develop and execute customized solutions. Employees get the opportunity to work in a challenging, rewarding, and caring environment. Shareholders receive above-market returns on their investment. The community gets a corporate citizen that operates with the public's safety foremost in mind, that protects the environment, and that participates in activities that improve the quality of life.

A company must realize that the needs of the four stakeholders are related and mutually supportive. Doing good for the community increases employees' pride in the company. Employees' participation in charitable activities supported by the company makes them feel good about themselves. Customers and shareholders like to be associated with companies that are forward thinking and take the initiative to address major societal issues. That is why I am ending this book by mentioning several highly innovative ways that FedEx is facing critical energy-related issues.

Since FedEx flies hundreds of planes every day, has tens of thousands of vehicles on the road, and operates hundreds of facilities around the world, it has a serious interest in conserving energy and reducing emissions. Recently, the company announced that it will construct California's largest corporate solar electric system atop its hub at Oakland International Airport. The 904-kilowatt solar array will provide approximately 80 percent of the facility's peak load demand.

FedEx is also testing diesel-electric hybrid delivery vehicles that use 50 percent less fuel than conventional vehicles and reduce emissions by 90 percent. Finally, FedEx took the lead in supporting the Airbus A380, which will become the largest aircraft in the air when it takes off in 2006. The cargo version that FedEx will operate uses 40 percent less fuel than the planes it will replace.

It is hard to justify all these energy-saving initiatives solely on the basis of traditional ROI calculations. But looking ahead, it is clear that companies must become more energy efficient. By adopting innovative, energy-saving technologies, FedEx is ensuring that it will continue to lead the way and outperform the competition well into the future.

Just as FedEx's leaders look ahead to the distant horizon and keep innovating to get there, so must the leaders of all businesses, large and small. By engaging employees in the enterprise, helping them grow all the time, creating a secure environment, encouraging collaboration, and tapping employees' commitment, anyone can create a culture of innovation and performance. This approach is the key to having a profitable and prosperous company.

Bibliography

Ally, Carl, quoted in *Wisdom Inc.* by Seth Godin, Harper Business, New York, 1995, p. 22.

AMA Management Briefing, "Blueprints for Service Quality: The Federal Express Approach," New York, 1991.

Bo Peabody, Co-founder and Chairman, Village Ventures, interviewed by Christine Canabou, "Books That Matter," *Fast Company*, April 2002, p. 48.

Botstein, Leon, "U1," *Fast Company*, October 2000, p. 104.

Boyle, Matthew, "Why FedEx Is Flying High," *Fortune*, October 8, 2004, p. 145.

Briscoe, James, "FedEx Courier in Boston, MA," *Fast Company*, March 2000, p. 110.

Broder, David S., *Washington Post*, April 17, 2003.

The CalTrade Report, Vol. 2, No. 5, November 1–15, 2004.

Cerf, Vinton, "U1," *Fast Company*, April 2000, p. 106.

Cribbin, James, Leadership Strategies for Organizational Effectiveness, AMACOM, New York, 1981.

Executive Briefing, *HR Magazine*, December 2001.

FedEx 2002 Annual Report.

FedEx 2003 Annual Report

FedEx 2004 Annual Report.

Fiorina, Carly, *Siliconindia* magazine, August 2001, p. 34.

Fisher, Anne, "Fortune Best Business Books," *Fortune*, May 15, 2000.

Fujita,Tony, "U1," *Fast Company*, March 2000, p. 118.

"Great Ideas Abound, But Implementation Lags," Executive Briefing, *HR Magazine*, March 2003, p. 14.

Hamel, Gary, "The American Paradox," *Fortune*, November 12, 2001.

Hammer, Michael, and Steven Stanton, "The Power of Reflection," *Fortune*, November 24, 1997, p. 296.

Holstein, Bill, CEO of the Year interview, September 2004, www.chiefexecutive.net.

"How Time Flies: FedEx Delivers the 21st Century," A FedEx in-house publication celebrating its first 25 years, Memphis, TN, 1998.

IBM Ad, *Fortune*, August 9, 2004.

Kahneman, Daniel, *Fast Company*, January 2003, p. 20.

Kanter, Rosabeth Moss, *The Change Masters*, New York: Simon & Schuster, 1983, Chapter 1, p. 20.

Kets de Vries, F. R., "Life and Death in the Executive Fast Lane," book review by Harry Levinson *Harvard Business Review*, January/February 1996.

Maslow, Abraham, *Motivation and Persomality*, 2nd ed., New York: Harper & Row, 1970.

Minton, Lynn, *Parade* magazine, June 2, 2001.

"The New Blue," Cover Story, *BusinessWeek* online, March 17, 2003.

Nyberg, Lars, *Fast Company*, October 2001, p. 76.

Orecklin, Michael, "Stress and the Superdad," *Time*, August 23, 2004.

Ruettgers, Mike, "Outside the Box," CBS Marketwatch.com, November 21, 2001.

Schlender, Brent, Cover Story, *Fortune*, July 20, 1998, p. 55.

Sellers, Patricia, Innovation Special section, *Fortune*, May 31, 2004, p. 148.

Smith, Fred, From the Chief Executive Officer, June 2000.

Smith, Fred, J. D. Power and Associates Customer Service Conference, Santa Monica, CA, November 13, 2003.

Stewart, Thomas, "Just Think: No Permission Needed," *Fortune*, January 8, 2001, p. 192.

Stewart, Thomas, A., "A Conversation with Joseph Juran," *Fortune*, January 11, 1999, p. 170.

Tobias, Randall, CEO, Eli Lilly and Company, Alliance of Work/Life Professionals Annual Conference, 1996.

Tobias, Randall, Interviewed by Peter Haapaniemi for *Unisys Exec* magazine, Vol. 25, No. 2, 2003, p. 12.

"Two of the 10 Rules of Growth from THQ," *Fast Company*, October 2000, p. 308.

Watson, Anne, Letter to the Editors, *IONS Noetic Sciences Review*, May 2001, p. 3.

Wye, Saw Ken, Manging Director, Microsoft, Singapore, *Fast Company*, September 1999.

Zander, Ed, *Business 2.0*, July 2003, p. 30.

Index

From Reading to Reality

To meet the challenges of today's highly competitive global marketplace, leaders at all levels in the organization must learn how to **build and sustain an innovation and performance culture,** the key to tapping employees' creativity and commitment.

As a strategic partner, Innovation Culture Group provides you with a wide-range of customized training and consulting services including organizational and leadership assessments, in-depth analyses, actionable recommendations, and ongoing implementation support at all levels of the organization.

Some of the proven products and services we offer are

- Web-based organizational "Innovation and Performance Culture" assessment
- Web-based individual manager "Leading for Innovation and Performance" assessment
- Classes and coaching to enhance high potential managers' strategic and business thinking skills
- Speakers for management meetings and planning sessions
  - Creating Competitive Advantage through Innovation and Performance
  - Transforming Successful Technical/Analytical Managers into Inspiring Leaders
  - Leading for Innovation and Life Balance, a Nurturing Relationship

For more information and to contact us, please visit:

www.Innovation**Culture**.com

Innovation Culture Group

Partner in Enhancing Your Competitive Edge